IF SHE IS RAPED:
A Book For Husbands, Fathers and Male Friends

Consulting Editor
Human Services Series

Edsel L. Erickson

Western Michigan University

IF SHE IS RAPED:
A Book For Husbands, Fathers And Male Friends

Alan W. McEvoy
Jeff B. Brookings
Wittenberg University

LP LEARNING PUBLICATIONS, INC.
Holmes Beach, FL 33509

Library of Congress Number: 83-83180

Learning Publications, Inc.
PO Box 1326
Holmes Beach, Florida 33509

Softcover: ISBN 0-918452-71-6

Cover Design by Barbara J. Wirtz

Printing: 2 3 4 5 6 7 8   Year: 5 6 7 8 9

Printed and bound in the United States of America

Acknowledgments

We wish to express our deepest gratitude to the staff of Project Woman of Springfield, Ohio, for their kind cooperation. We would like to give special thanks to Joy Thomas, Rose Tingley, Chris Myers, Sally Shears, Judy Jones, Danna Downing and Edsel Erickson for their insightful contributions. We would also like to thank Janice McEvoy and Allison Brookings for their love and continued support throughout this endeavor. Finally, we wish to thank all those who work with rape victims; it is to those helpers that this book is dedicated.

Table of Contents

Preface

This book will give husbands, fathers and male friends of rape victims an understanding of the dynamics of rape from the woman's point of view, and will suggest practical ways for you to help in her recovery. We will help you understand what happens from the time of the rape until well after the possible rape trial. Furthermore, we will suggest what you should and should not do when relating to a victim and others close to her. Finally, this book will help you deal with your own feelings about the rape incident and its consequences, as well as provide you with the emotional tools to maintain a healthy relationship with those you love.

1
Understanding Rape

Forcible rape is an act of sexual violence that is usually accompanied by physical threat, nearly always done to females by males, without the woman's consent. Rape is a disturbingly frequent type of crime. The FBI estimates that in the United States alone, there are about 240 rapes per day, or nearly 88,000 per year. Since rape so often goes unreported, most experts agree that these statistics are at best a conservative estimate of the actual number of rapes occurring each year.

During the past decade, rape has become the topic of numerous research studies, newspaper stories, and TV documentaries. The women's movement in particular has focused attention on the traumatic nature of rape, the reasons for such acts of violence against women, and the role of the criminal justice system in dealing with rape. As a result of these efforts, public awareness concerning the seriousness of rape has been enhanced, the criminal justice system has begun to deal with rape as more than just a minor crime, and hundreds of rape crisis centers have been established to assist women who are victimized by sexual assault.

As might be expected, most of the resources of rape crisis centers, investigative units in police departments and counseling facilities are directed toward providing assistance to the woman who is raped. However, rape is a crime that deeply affects not only the woman, but also family members and other loved ones. Because of the violent and sexual nature of rape, men who are significant others to the victim—husbands, fathers and male friends—usually have a particularly difficult time coming to terms with her victimization and providing her with the necessary emotional support. By understanding the nature and consequences of rape, men who are close to the rape victim can play a crucial role in helping her deal with the short-term and long-term consequences of this traumatic life event.

Facts and Myths About Rape

There is no such thing as a "typical" rape or rape victim. Certainly each episode represents a unique and terrifying experience in the life of the woman. However, there are a number of common elements as well as misconceptions associated with rape; awareness of them may help sensitize you to what she has been through.

To begin, we cannot overstate the point that rape is not the same as "making love." Although the majority of rapes involve vaginal penetration, this is done in a state of emotional terror without the woman giving consent. It is a complete misconception to believe that women "secretly desire" to be raped or taken by force. Rape is a total violation of a woman's rights over her own body and of her ability to make a sexual choice. Indeed, from the woman's point of view, the sexual dimension of rape often assumes lesser importance than the violent aspects.

Rape is fundamentally an act of violence. Nearly all rapes involve threats of bodily harm, and in many cases the woman suffers severe physical injury. In fact, most rape victims report being pushed or "roughed up" by the rapist and about 90% receive some degree of physical injury. Threats of violence are made even worse by the presence of a weapon and intimidating verbal abuse. An act of rape means that the woman was violated not only physically, but psychologically as well through the use of violence and verbal degradation. Any implication that the woman "asked for" or enjoyed the experience, or that rape and making love are the same, is a basic misconception about the nature of rape.

A related fact concerning rape is that the woman is absolutely *not* responsible for her victimization. Men often mistakenly assume that she could have prevented the rape by avoiding certain social situations, dressing differently, or by putting up a fight. This mistaken suspicion may be even greater if the victim exhibits no visible physical injuries. The truth is that virtually anyone placed in a life threatening situation can be paralyzed by fear or recognize the futility of physical resistance. There is no way for a woman—indeed, for anyone—to completely guarantee the safety of an environment.

Moreover, as many rapes occur between casual acquaintances or friends as between total strangers. Likewise, rape occurs at all hours of the day or night and in virtually any setting. Frequently rape occurs in one's own home or in a public place. Believing that the woman is partially responsible for the rape incident is not only a mistaken assumption, but an assumption that will place emotional distance between the two of you at a time when the need for emotional support is greatest. Such an assumption may cause unnecessary feelings of guilt, anger and isolation. Ultimately, placing blame on her will prolong her recovery process and add great strain to your relationship with her.

Finally, it is important to realize that rape can happen to anyone, regardless of age, income, appearance or personal "reputation." However, it is true that the majority of rape victims are single women between the ages of 12 and 24. Nevertheless, there is no way to predict which women are likely to be selected as victims. The one feature common to all rapes is that it is a frightening and degrading experience that usually requires a period of time in which to recover emotionally. Furthermore, we know that men close to the victim also are affected deeply by the rape of a loved one, that men can learn to understand a woman's victimization, and that the husbands, fathers or male friends of rape victims can act in a manner that contributes to her recovery.

How You Can Help

You can begin to reduce the harm to the victim and those she loves:

1. **by knowing** what to expect from her and others following the rape;

2. **by recognizing and accepting** her feelings, as well as your own and others close to her;

3. **by communicating** to her a sense of compassion and acceptance;

4. **by sharing** with her so that she senses that she is not alone and that she has your unconditional love and support.

Remember, rape is a violent crime that is neither sought nor caused by the victim. While your feelings are important, helping her to recover should be your first concern.

2
Dealing With
Immediate Concerns

The period immediately following a rape is likely to be an emotionally charged, confusing and extremely anxious time for the victim. Not only has she been terrorized and totally violated as a person, but she now is faced with many additional worries. For example, directly following the rape, victims typically consider such questions as:

"Do I need medical attention?"

"Do I report this to the police?"

"Am I pregnant?"

"Did I contract venereal disease?"

"Should I tell my family?"

"What will others think of me?"

"Will he attempt to rape me again?"

Obviously, the emotional consequences of rape continue well beyond the experience itself. Unfortunately, doctors, police and lawyers often unintentionally contribute to the problem as they carry out their bureaucratic routines in hospitals and police departments. For example, if the victim decides to immediately report the rape to the police, she is required to undergo a series of medical exams—for legal reasons—*before* she has the opportunity to bathe and change clothing. This may entail a lengthy wait in a hospital emergency room followed by a series of medical examinations. This medical evidence is essential for future legal action and will be discussed in detail in Chapter 8.

In the process of providing evidence to the police, the woman is required to undergo lengthy interviews where she may have to recount the rape several times in detail to strangers (usually men). In addition, she is required to examine "mug" shots or help construct composite sketches of the rapist, and perhaps submit to a polygraph exam. Because polygraph evidence is not necessarily admissible in court, she may refuse to take the test. However, she may request to take the test in order to further establish the credibility of her story.

While it is true that rules of evidence require detailed questioning by police, the examination procedures may appear to her as unnecessary and an invasion of her privacy. These lengthy procedures occur at a time when the woman already feels mentally and physically debased. At the very moment she most needs sympathetic understanding, impersonal routines add to an already heavy emotional burden.

Even if she chooses not to report the incident to the police, she still should be examined by a physician. In the first place, she may require immediate medical attention. In addition, if she changes her mind and decides to report the rape, she will need medical evidence to take legal action. Finally, because pregnancy and venereal disease tests do not yield immediate results, she will need to return to the physician approximately three weeks after the rape to take these tests.

The period of time immediately following the rape requires great care and emotional support. It is at this critical period that you can help set in motion the psychological forces that will contribute to her recovery. How and what you communicate to her is of paramount importance in determining how she interprets the rape incident and how she feels about herself. Specifically, there are a number of things you should and should not do when you first learn that someone you love has been raped.

Do's and Don'ts

- A common initial reaction among men is a strong desire to seek revenge against the rapist. However, this is a time when calm and reasoned judgments are most needed. It is especially important that you do not personally contact the rapist, even if his identity is known to you. Such actions can create legal problems for you and place the woman in the position of having to deal with additional fears concerning your safety. In fact, making verbal threats toward the rapist in the presence of the victim is likely to intensify the fear and anxiety she is already feeling.

- Related to a desire for revenge, when men first learn of the rape they usually experience an intense sense of anger coupled with frustration. Most males feel a desire to "strike back" but have no one to whom this anger can be directed. Such powerful emotions, while understandable, can be destructive unless properly channeled. For instance, in no way should such turbulent feelings be directed toward the woman. In fact, upon first encountering her you should refrain from venting your frustrations. The thing she may want and need most at that time is simply to be held and spoken to with gentleness. Under no circumstances should you accuse her or judge her in any way. It is important for you to remain calm and give her the opportunity, if she desires, to discuss the experience. While your feelings are important, how she feels needs to be your primary concern.

•   In addition, it is essential you communicate to her that she is not responsible for being raped. Do not ask her questions like "Why didn't you scream and run? Why were you at that place at that time? Why did you talk to him in the first place?" Such questions as these only make her feel guilty and possibly even resentful toward you. She needs to know that you do not blame her for failing to resist the rapist or for being in a situation that resulted in rape.

•   Not only should you avoid implying cooperation on her part, but you absolutely should avoid suggesting that she secretly may have enjoyed the experience. Rape is a violent and frequently painful act that is not a source of pleasure for the victim. It is important for her to feel reassured that you do

not equate her rape with an act of infidelity or promiscuity, and that you do not see her as defiled or
less moral than prior to the incident. The ability
to feel and communicate unconditional love and acceptance toward the woman is an important first
step in reducing the deep sense of anxiety she may
feel.

- Just as many males accept as true some of the myths
  and stereotypes about rape, so too do many women.
  When she is ready, encourage her to discuss any
  beliefs or assumptions about rape that perhaps are
  contributing to her emotional state. Convince her
  that you do not share those views which place the
  woman at fault.

- Sexual assault robs the woman of a sense of control over her life. Feelings of loss of control over
  one's own body and loss of freedom are common
  among rape victims. In order for her to work
  through the trauma of the rape and begin to put her
  life back in order, she must regain this sense of control. Therefore, it is important that the woman be
  encouraged to make decisions about any and all
  events which affect her life (e.g., whether to report
  the crime, go to trial, tell family and friends, seek
  counseling, etc.). Do not attempt to make these
  decisions for her or demand that she follow a particular course of action, even though you quite
  naturally want to help her and feel more useful
  yourself by "taking charge" of the situation.

- It is important for you to communicate your un-
  failing support for her in whatever decisions she

makes. She needs to feel that no matter what she decides, you will stick by her and that there will continue to be love, security and constancy in your relationship with her. Furthermore, communicate to her that you will actively encourage support and cooperation from family and friends who know of the incident.

- Don't expect or demand immediate, open communication with the victim regarding how she feels or the vivid details of the rape. At this point, she may not have had sufficient time to sort out her feelings, or she may wish to guard her feelings due to a deep-seated sense of embarrassment. It is particularly important that you refrain from prying into the sexually intimate aspects of the rape or force her to self-disclose what is, to her, the ultimate humiliation. Accept the fact that she will discuss with you her feelings when she is ready.

- Finally, she needs to feel that she is not alone. It is important for her to know that others have endured similar events and that regardless of what happened, your love and support remain intact.

3
Talking With
The Victim and Others

For the rape victim, having to relate the incident to you and to other significant persons in her life can be a major source of emotional conflict and anxiety. Effective communication between the victim and those close to her is very important to her long-term adjustment and to the survival of her significant relationships.

What To Say To The Victim

Given the emotional turmoil you both are experiencing, there are several steps you can take to promote effective communication between yourself and the victim:

- Be a patient, approachable and effective listener. Being an effective listener requires sensitivity to her feelings and a willingness to demonstrate unconditional acceptance of her. By giving her the

opportunity to express her feelings when she is
ready, you will help her work through emotional
conflicts and will yourself gain a better understanding of what she is going through.

• Don't pressure her. When she is ready to discuss
her feelings with you, she will do so. Until then,
attempting to force her to discuss her feelings can
intensify her confusion and anxiety, may make her
withdraw, and may also make her resent you.

• Pay special attention to recurring themes she raises
with you in conversation. These topics might be
clues which will provide insight into issues which
are especially troublesome to her. Being victimized
by rape can bring to the forefront of her consciousness much "unfinished business" that has
long troubled her. By being alert to her conversa-
tional themes and by being open to discuss sensitive
issues, you may come to better understand her
emotional state and help her to resolve long-standing
difficulties.

• At some point in time, it is important for the two
of you to discuss the impact of the rape on your
relationship. The emotional consequences of rape
are traumatic for all those involved in a personal
relationship with the woman, including you. It is
neither possible nor constructive for you to suppress
indefinitely your reactions to the rape of a loved
one. Sharing your feelings and vulnerabilities with
her affords her the opportunity to nurture you, just
as you have been nurturing her. Nurturing another
person is an effective way to overcome one's own
difficulties, thus aiding the recovery process.

- Consider relationship counseling for the two of you. Many rape crisis centers provide such services at little or no cost. A competent, sensitive counselor can help you identify and remove barriers to effective communication.

What To Say To Others

In the aftermath of a rape, family members often have responses which parallel those of the woman: shock, rage, confusion, feelings of helplessness, etc. It is important that family members have an opportunity to express their feelings and demonstrate their concern and support for the victim. However, well-intentioned efforts which create additional emotional burdens for her must be prevented. You may find yourself in the position of being a "buffer" between the woman and other members of her family. If so, the following hints can help you deal with this situation:

- Family members may seek to help the victim and alleviate their own feelings of helplessness by threatening revenge on the rapist. When discussed in the presence of the victim, such threats tend to further traumatize the woman and cause her to worry about the safety of her family. Family members' anger can be expressed verbally, perhaps to you or a family counselor, but should not be expressed in the presence of the victim. Constant expression of anger and frustration only serves to heighten her anxieties and confusion about the incident. She may even feel guilty for "imposing" such an emotional burden on those she loves.

- Family members may try to solicit support for the woman from close friends, clergy, co-workers, and others. Such efforts should be discouraged if the woman is not prepared to discuss the incident or chooses to discuss it with only a few people. This does not mean, however, that you should prevent her from self-disclosing to others, such as family members, if she so chooses.

- Family members should be dissuaded from over-protecting the victim. Strong attempts may be made to convince her to move back home, move to another city, or accept what amounts to 24 hour surveillance by the family. The danger is that these actions may reinforce the woman's view of herself as vulnerable and powerless. The unintended result may be to discourage her from mobilizing her own resources for coping with the situation, thus promoting an unhealthy dependency on others. Providing support should not function to increase feelings that she has lost control over her life or that she is no longer self-reliant. If anything, family members need to understand that being supportive in part means helping her to build self-confidence and independence.

- Continual "distraction" of the woman by family members and friends should be discouraged. The family may engage in a "friendly conspiracy" to keep her mind off the incident by occupying her time with a variety of activities. They may even act as if it never happened. However, attempts to deny or repress the rape are only temporarily effective and communicate to the victim that the incident is too awful to discuss or even think about. Such behavior only slows down her attempts to express and work through her emotional reactions.

- Be sensitive to the woman's need for privacy. There are times when it is desirable and therapeutic for her to work through her feelings alone. A constant stream of well-wishers, even if they are family, can further drain her emotionally. It is especially difficult for her to put the incident behind her if she feels obliged to satisfy the frequent inquiries of visitors as to "what happened" and "how are you doing." When she decides she needs to be alone, respect that decision. In addition, she may want you to communicate such decisions to the family for her. In doing so, you can assure the family and friends that their concern is both recognized and appreciated.

- Finally, all should work together to provide a safe, accepting climate into which the woman can release painful feelings without fear of judgment or criticism.

4
Responding to Long Term Consequences

We have described the woman's experience of rape and its immediate impact upon her. By now, however, it should be apparent that the effects of rape on her extend far beyond the episode and its immediate aftermath. A complete resolution of the incident may take months or even years for her to achieve. As time passes, there are a number of physical and psychological responses for which you should be prepared.

It was mentioned earlier that there is no such thing as a "typical" rape or rape victim. Likewise, there is no such thing as a "typical" pattern of responses to rape. Some victims may express their feelings quite openly, while others attempt to control and hide them. Despite these individual differences, however, many counselors report that their clients' responses to rape follow a sequence referred to as the "Rape Trauma Syndrome." This "syndrome" is *not* a type of mental disorder, but a series of stages many (but not all) rape victims experience.

The first phase, acute distress, begins with the woman's responses to the rape in the hours immediately following the incident. These immediate responses may include shock, disbelief, confusion, anxiety, crying, and other signs of emotional disorganization. She may even appear to be extremely controlled on the surface, masking more troubling emotions at a deeper level. At the same time, a number of physical symptoms may appear over a period of several weeks following the rape: soreness and bruising from the attack, vaginal or rectal bleeding, tension headaches and fatigue, sleep disturbances (e.g., nightmares, insomnia, inability to go back to sleep after awakening, crying out in her sleep), stomach pains, nausea and lack of appetite, vaginal infection, and difficulty in urinating. Since antipregnancy and antivenereal disease medications are often prescribed when vaginal penetration occurs, some of the physical symptoms described above may be side effects of the medication.

Emotionally, the victim experiences a variety of feelings in the weeks following the rape: fear, anger, embarrassment, and self-blame. Abrupt changes in mood are quite common. If circumstances surrounding the rape (such as the place it occurred) are similar to aspects of the victim's everyday world, she will be constantly reminded of the incident, and her emotional responses may be even more intense. To compound her distress, the woman may feel she is overreacting to various everyday problems and get angry with herself over her own behavior. Let her know that her emotional reactions to the assault are understandable and do *not* mean she is "going crazy" or is neurotic.

During this first phase, it is particularly important for you to remember that these physical and emotional reactions are *natural* responses to a terrifying, life-threatening experience.

Be prepared to offer the kind of support *she* needs and let her convey to you what her needs are. When she asks to be held, hold her. When she asks to be left alone, leave her alone and see that family and friends leave her alone as well. Let her know that you are available when she needs you, but let her know also that you have faith in her ability to work through these difficult times.

The second phase, a period of *apparent* readjustment, is an outgrowth of the first phase. That is, the woman may attempt to resolve her anxiety and confusion by rationalizing the rape and her feelings about it. For example, she may announce that she has ''forgotten'' the incident and give every outward appearance that the rape no longer troubles her. This may appear to be a final resolution, but typically is not. If anything, the rape incident is constantly in the background of her thoughts and has not been resolved. Keep in mind that this second phase *does* represent another step towards a true resolution of the incident.

The third phase, called reorganization or integration, is marked by emergence or reemergence of a number of troubling responses experienced earlier. For example, depression, anxiety, fear, insomnia, nightmares, and various physical symptoms (e.g., stomach pain, tension headaches, etc.) are common. She may also cry unexpectedly and want to talk about the rape. Her emotional turmoil will surface in response to everyday tension in ways that are disquieting and perhaps unpredictable. Many relationships undergo the greatest period of stress at this time because she appears to be ''getting worse instead of better.'' These responses, while understandably disturbing to both of you, are actually a sign that she is beginning to confront and grapple with deep-seated feelings about the rape, feelings which she previously denied or rationalized.

Unfortunately, many victims incorrectly blame themselves for the rape. A period of guilt and self-blame is common even though the rape could not have been prevented. Many rapists spend considerable time "stalking" their victims, waiting for an opportune moment when she is least able to resist. In order to help her deal with feelings of self-blame, it is important to convey to her four simple truisms about rape:

1. Regardless of where a woman is, no one has the right to rape her.

2. The fact that she may have been alone, dressed in a particular way, or been friendly to a person does not mean she deserved to be raped.

3. She is never responsible for the behavior of a rapist.

4. Most important, the fact that she survived the rape means that she did the right thing.

In addition, strong feelings of anger towards the rapist, feelings which perhaps were denied or repressed during the period of apparent readjustment, may surface at this time. It is important for her to express this anger. By offering continued comfort, support, reassurance and understanding, you and other family members can provide an environment in which she can safely vent and cope with her feelings.

Recently, rape crisis counselors have pointed out that male significant others of rape victims also pass through a series of phases, similar to those of the victim's Rape Trauma Syndrome. As a result, they too need to achieve resolution of the incident. For males, however, an initial phase of guilt and self-blame for failing to protect her is quickly followed by intense anger and frustration. As was said earlier, since venting your anger in the presence of the victim may further traumatize her, you should seek out a good friend or counselor with whom to release pent-up emotional energy. At the same time, it is important that you and your loved one let each know what the other is feeling.

We also stress that your feelings, however intense, are not unusual. Many males whose loved ones have been raped feel a kind of "impotent rage"—wanting to strike out but having no appropriate means to do so. Your feelings of anger are natural and a common reaction among men. However, your feelings about the incident should be expressed to her in a gentle and calm manner, rather than in a state of extreme agitation or rage. This will keep the lines of communication open, a factor which is critical for the survival of your relationship with her.

Remember also that each person has developed his or her own strategies for coping with emotional stress. Although you should share your feelings with each other, don't expect her methods of coping to be identical with yours. Allow her the freedom to adjust in her own way and do not be upset if her feelings or actions are not the same as yours.* While no two people recover in the same way, with mutual support and openness, you both will recover.

Finally, difficult as it may be, you must realize that resolution of the incident does not necessarily mean that "things will be the way they always were." In fact, "resolution" of the rape means that she has come to terms with her victimization,

---

*We strongly recomend that she read a companion volume to this book written specifically for rape victims. The book is entitled *If You Are Raped*, by Kathryn M. Johnson, Learning Publications, Inc., 1984.

but it also means that her view of herself and possibly her relationships with others are significantly changed. At the same time, by being supportive, patient, and caring, you may succeed in building a relationship with her which is even *stronger* than before.

5
Overcoming Fears About Sex

One of the consequences of rape is considerable anxiety concerning sexual activity. For a young victim, rape may be her first sexual experience and thus cause great confusion about the nature of human sexuality. For all victims, rape is done in a violent context devoid of love and emotional intimacy. Such an experience may result in a long-term fear of sexual involvement or increase sexual difficulties that already existed between partners. In the case of child victims, even if there are no immediate difficulties in adjustment, the experience may be repressed and surface at a later point in life. It is very important that one or both parents or a counselor patiently explain about the nature of human intimacy, openly answering all questions she might have. Fear of sexual intimacy is likely to be compounded in the absence of information.

For men who are the sexual partners of rape victims, there is likely to be a temporary disruption in previous patterns of sexual activity. Sexual difficulties may be especially acute if the rape was extremely violent or involved multiple rapists.

For a period of time, most sexually active victims experience changes in sexual responsiveness and in the frequency of sexual behavior. They are often confronted with deep-seated concerns over the resumption of sexual relations, as well as their sexual responses and the responses of their partners.

The lack of understanding or the insensitivity of a victim's partner may make the resumption of sexual activity seem rapelike, or provide her with cues that remind her of the incident. It is not uncommon for a victim to experience flashbacks of the rape during sexual relations with her partner. Likewise, males are often insecure about their sexual performance with a woman who has been raped, especially if she seems reluctant or unresponsive. Both males and females normally experience complex feelings about their own sexual impulses following a rape. As her partner, you should ask yourself, "How can I effectively communicate with the woman I love when she has been sexually victimized by another man?" To address this issue, keep in mind the following suggestions.

- In the aftermath of rape, the woman needs to be given every opportunity to regain her sense of personal control, especially in the area of sexual decision making. Remember that rape removes a woman's power of sexual choice, the one arena where many expect women to display moral integrity and self-control.

- Do not demand or pressure her into sexual activity immediately after the episode. Resuming sex is not the psychological equivalent of "getting back on the horse after falling off." Let her take control of sexual decision making during her recovery. Many women prefer a period of sexual abstinence after being raped. As one rape victim reported: "In the first couple of weeks, it was good enough just to be close...didn't have to do anything physical. He was patient...after the initial feeling of aversion died away, it was me who wanted it."[1] Being responsive to her needs and respecting her decisions will go a long way toward overcoming sexual problems.

• Don't be angry with her or doubt your own sexual adequacy if she appears less sexually responsive than previously. Sexual fears are likely to reduce sexual desire. It may be that certain cues present during the rape (e.g., the smell of alcohol) inhibit later sexual responsiveness. Give her the opportunity to openly communicate to you her feelings about your sexual relationship. Feelings of anger, frustration, or an unwillingness to alter certain patterns are likely to distance you from her and place an added burden on your sexual relationship.

• Some males experience erotic feelings when the victim describes the rape to them, and then feel guilty for having such feelings. This merely demonstrates the fact that rape produces a variety of conflicting emotions in people. If you do feel aroused when learning of the incident, *do not* communicate these feelings to the victim because it will only provoke greater anxiety in her. Unfortunately, many males tend to dwell on the sexual aspects

---

[1]Burgess, Ann and Holstrom, Lynda; "RAPE: SEXUAL DISRUPTION AND RECOVERY," *American Journal of Orthopsychiatry*, October, 1979, p. 49(4).

of her victimization and forget that rape is primarily
an act of violence. If such feelings persist, it would
be valuable to seek the assistance of a counselor.

- Be patient. Sexual disruption following rape is
  usually temporary and can be overcome with sensitivity and understanding.

A Special Word To Fathers

When the victim of sexual assault is a child or adolescent, the emotional impact on her and her family is especially
severe. Fathers, who have a strong sense of responsibility for
the safety of their daughters, may have particularly strong reactions such as rage and self-blame. In the crucial hours and
days following the rape, however, it is absolutely critical that
you be aware of the stresses that your child will yet have to
endure, and what you can do to lessen their impact on her.
The following should be kept in mind:

- If the crime is reported to the authorities and the
  victim is age 16 or under, parental permission is
  required for medical treatment and police questioning. Be available to provide such authorizations and
  any additional information needed by medical and
  police personnel.

- The rape may have been your daughter's first sexual experience. Because of this, her fears about
  adult intimacy are usually exaggerated. She needs
  to know that she is not tarnished by the experience,
  that her capacity for sexual intimacy in adulthood
  is not diminished, and that rape is not how loving
  couples express themselves sexually.

- The gynecological exam she must undergo may also be a first-time experience and can be extremely upsetting unless parents and medical staff are sensitive to what she is going through. Since hospitals may be held legally accountable for failing to examine a victim, and since medical evidence would be needed in the event of a trial, you must gently convince your daughter that the procedure is necessary; however, you should insist also that the medical staff carry out the exam with patience and sensitivity.

- A common response on the part of fathers is to "blame someone" for the crime. We have already pointed out that blaming the victim or making threats of revenge against the rapist are counter-productive and should be avoided. We want to emphasize again that you should not hold yourself responsible for the rape or for failing to protect her. It is virtually impossible to create an environment in which the possibility of rape is completely eliminated. Instead of worrying about who is to blame for the incident, concentrate your energy on helping your daughter to a complete physical and emotional recovery.

- If the victim is an adolescent, the rape may compound communication problems which often already exist between parents and daughters. This may make it doubly difficult for her to speak with you about the rape and her reactions to it. If so, do not force her to self-disclose to you or anyone else. However, if she expresses a desire to talk about the assault with you or other family members, be prepared to do so. We believe that rape victims benefit from talking about the experience, if it is *their* decision to talk about it. Attempts to help her "forget" about the rape by refusing to discuss it may give her the impression that you are ashamed of her or in some way hold her responsible for being raped. A family counselor may be helpful in developing more effective communication between yourself and your daughter, as well as other family members, so that each will gain a better understanding of what the others are feeling.

•   If the victim is a young child, she may express her reactions behaviorally, rather than verbally. Be alert for changes such as loss of appetite, withdrawal from social contact, altered sleeping patterns, frequent nightmares, avoidance of strangers, or fear of being alone. These reactions are quite common in the weeks and months following the rape, but should be monitored closely for frequency and severity.

•   Encourage your daughter to resume her normal lifestyle as soon as possible. Limiting your daughter's emerging independence by making decisions for her, or "grounding" her for not being sufficiently careful, may seem like punishment to her and should be avoided. It is important that her rights concerning dating, seeing friends, involvement in extracurricular events at school, as well as her responsibilities for household chores, remain the same. If she is overprotected or allowed to avoid routine activities, she will have a more lengthy and difficult period of readjustment.

6
Understanding Acquaintance Rape

Although statistics vary, the best estimates suggest that approximately half of all rape victims are attacked by someone they know. Obviously the nature of the victim-offender relationship exists on a continuum from slight acquaintance to former husband or lover. In a great many cases, rape occurs in the context of a dating relationship or, if a child is the victim, within the family. While adult victims over age 25 have a somewhat greater likelihood of being raped by a total stranger, children, adolescents and college age females are most likely to be victimized by a person who is known. The occurrence of acquaintance rape tends to complicate the legal and emotional consequences for the victim and those who love her.

While rape by a total stranger is traumatic and frightening, assault by someone who is known and trusted may be even more devastating. Consider the situation of many teenagers and college students whose active social lives regularly involve them in school activities, parties and other settings where they are in contact with a variety of males. There is a tendency among females to assume that such settings are a safe way of meeting new friends and potential dating partners. In such encounters, where she comes to know someone at least casually, it is normal and understandable to presume a certain degree of trust and to want to be on good terms. As a consequence of her good intentions and a desire to be sociable, her trust is used against her and she is placed at great risk.

The following sequence of events seems typical of the dynamics involved in many cases of acquaintance rape. A young woman is introduced to a "friend of a friend" at a party. Since he appears to her to be "a decent guy," she accepts his invitation to go out for something to eat. Because she has no reason to suspect his motives, she invites him into her apartment for an after-dinner drink. Whether misinterpreting her friendliness or because of more sinister motives, the man makes physical advances toward her. Not wanting to seem rude, the woman politely puts up with his initial advances and gently tries to dissuade him. Her desire to spare his feelings and the belief that she can control the situation actually work to her disadvantage as she delays taking any protective action. As his behavior becomes progressively more unacceptable and aggressive, she finally becomes insistent and demands that he stop. It is at this point that the man typically becomes verbally abusive (e.g., calling her a "bitch" or a "tease") and escalates to the use of physical force to impose his will upon her.

Unfortunately, episodes of this nature occur at an alarming rate in the context of dating relationships. Given such an experience, not only has the woman become the victim of a sexual assault, but she is often left with a lingering feeling that she is somehow responsible for using poor judgment or for failing to control his ''natural urges.'' Little wonder that victims of acquaintance rape characteristically experience great confusion and strong feelings of guilt. It is also not surprising that victims of this form of sexual assault are *least* likely to report it to the police. In part, her confusion stems from widely held beliefs in our culture that after a certain degree of intimacy (e.g., kissing, petting, etc.), males have sexual rights over a woman regardless of her objections. Thus the burden is placed on the female to recognize at what point *he* can no longer control *his* ''urges,'' implying that she is responsible for his aggressiveness and lack of self-control.

The psychological effects of acquaintance rape on the victim may be somewhat different than the emotions accompanying rape by a complete stranger. We do not mean to imply that the consequences are less serious. If anything, some of the emotional consequences are likely to be felt *more* intensely in cases where the victim and offender are known to one another. Because she has been violated by someone she trusted, she may now believe that she is a poor judge of character. It is common for these victims to experience a sense of self-doubt and a feeling of apprehension, especially when encountering unfamiliar people. This lack of faith in her powers of judgment may gradually develop into a generalized distrust of *all* males, including close friends.

In addition, the victim may feel that by not refusing his advances sooner or more firmly, she somehow bears partial responsibility for ''triggering'' in him these ''uncontrollable'' desires. Such deeply felt confusion over her judgment and responsibility is intensified by mutual friends who claim that ''he's not that kind of guy.'' In many cases the victim is cut off from the support of family and friends because she remains silent out of fear that others will not believe she was assaulted,

or worse, will claim that she provoked him. To the extent that
the rapist has friends and communication links within the same
social network as the victim, her potential support system is
likely to be undermined and her version of events called into
question. It is this lack of support that has negative consequences for her emotional adjustment and decreases the
likelihood of her pursuing legal action.

If the victim decides to take legal action against an assailant
who is known to her, the emotional difficulties she experiences
may be compounded. Police investigators frequently express
reluctance to pursue criminal cases where evidence is perceived
to be difficult to obtain or if they believe that charges will be
dropped when the case goes to trial. Because conclusive
evidence is often difficult to produce in rape investigations,
the police may view the victim's claim as unsubstantiated or
impossible to prove in court. Acquaintance rape, particularly
if it involves a former lover or ex-husband, is likely to be
dismissed by police as an "unfounded" charge and therefore
not worth the time and trouble to investigate. The reasons for
unfounding charges of rape against acquaintances include the
following:

1.   A tendency to view the reported episode as a
     "lover's quarrel" rather than as a serious sexual
     assault

2.   A belief that she will drop all charges after she has
     had time to "cool down"

3.   If kissing or sexual foreplay occurred prior to the
     assault, a belief that she "assumed the risk" and
     gave tacit consent to intercourse

4. A belief that the victim is promiscuous, a "pick-up," or that she intentionally was being seductive or a "tease"

5. Because of prior sexual involvement with the man (e.g., an ex-husband), a belief that she is exaggerating or lying in order to seek revenge

6. Lack of physical evidence, medical reports, or eye witness accounts wherein the charge of rape becomes her word against his

7. Character witnesses who know both parties and whose testimony might cast doubt on her version of events

In a very real sense, police response (or rather lack of response) to her claim that she was raped by an acquaintance further contributes to her victimization. Although more will be said about this in a separate chapter, actions taken by the police and courts frequently add to her frustration and anxiety. The tendency of others not to believe she was actually raped, that she is being untruthful or gave implied consent to the rapist, often function to increase her sense of guilt, confusion, and anger.

As a significant person in her life, there are several ways you can demonstrate your support and affection if she has been sexually assaulted by an acquaintance and decides to press charges against him.

• To counter the self-doubts about her ability to judge character, you must convince her of a simple fact—it is impossible to know in advance who will be a rapist. Neighbors, friends, fellow employees, new acquaintances, and former partners are all potential assailants and may need only the right opportunity for rape to occur.

• Remind her that even if she was friendly to the rapist, she absolutely is not responsible for causing him to "lose control." Demonstrations of affection and friendship on her part do not make her liable for his aggressive actions.

• It is important for you to diffuse the generalized feeling of distrust she may have developed. Such apprehension can function to isolate her and greatly hamper her future interactions with others. She needs to feel that her assailant is not representative of all males and that trust is an essential prerequisite for developing intimate relationships. Indeed, your relationship with her should illustrate the value of openness and trust.

• Finally, it is of vital importance that you reassure her that you believe her story, regardless of the actions of police or others who are aware of the incident.

The case of acquaintance rape is likely to produce particularly strong emotional reactions in you as well. If the rapist is an acquaintance or friend of yours, you probably will feel a violation of trust or question your own judgment of character. Moreover, husbands and male partners of the victim often have friends who operate in the same social circle as the rapist. This can be very awkward for you, the woman, and those mutual friends and acquaintances who wish to avoid "taking sides."

Furthermore, information about the rapist's version of events, the impact of the incident on him and his family if legal action is taken, as well as general gossip about the reputation of both rapist and victim may become frequent topics of conversation and continually confront you and her. This is especially true if the victim and assailant are still attending school.

As we have indicated elsewhere, it is totally inappropriate and even dangerous for you to personally seek revenge against the rapist, even if he is known to you and could be located without difficulty. In addition, because mutual acquaintances fail to take sides or because they remain on good terms with the assailant, it may create doubts in your mind as to what extent he is actually to blame. It is a sure bet that the rapist will have denied everything to those in contact with him. You might begin to think, "After all, if the people we know still think he is OK, maybe it didn't happen the way she said." Given such thinking, it is possible that you will feel that she is partially to blame or that he is a sexual rival.

While such thoughts are understandable, they represent a distorted view of what has actually taken place. Regardless of any gossip you may hear, your assessment of events should reflect the realization that she is the victim, not the perpetrator. Your love relationship with her, not casual contacts with others, should be the basis for understanding what has transpired. In short, don't let others inadvertently jeopardize the trust and understanding that is the basis of your relationship with her. In light of these complexities surrounding acquaintance rape, it would be helpful for you to keep in mind the points which follow.

- No woman wants to be forced into sexual relations. The rapist, even if he is an acquaintance, is not your rival.

- You cannot control what others think or say about the incident. Your belief in her and your support of her are what matters.

- Do not feel guilty if an element of doubt crosses your mind. Such thoughts are not unusual but almost certainly are based on false assumptions.

- Neither you nor the victim are in any way responsible for what happens to the assailant if charges are filed with the police. It is the responsibility of the courts to decide his fate, regardless of any pressure that parents or friends of the rapist may bring to bear upon the victim or you.

- Do not isolate yourself or her from your network of peers who perhaps are aware of the rape. Neither she nor you have any reason to feel shame, embarrassment or guilt. Remember that your true friends will be understanding and supportive when there is a personal crisis.

In summary, it is obvious that the process of victimization continues well after the act of rape. The consequences of acquaintance rape can compound the emotional difficulties for the victim as well as for you. However, rapid and effective recovery is possible to the extent that there exists honest and open communication between you and the victim.

7

Dealing With Interracial Rape

It has been estimated that from 7 to 35% of reported rapes are interracial (e.g., black male-white female, white male-black female). Most reported rapes involve black assailants and white victims. However, the key word is "reported." There is evidence that black women, perhaps out of a belief that the police will not conduct a vigorous investigation of the complaint, are unlikely to report rapes if the assailant is white.

In any event, interracial rape tends to evoke especially strong feelings of outrage from those close to the victim. If expressed in her presence, these feelings may further confuse and traumatize her. In addition, the victim's own responses to interracial rape often are organized around racial themes. If so, her psychological recovery may be further impeded. It is therefore important that you understand the dynamics of interracial rape. Be prepared to deal with reactions of the victim and those close to her which might hinder a healthy resolution of the incident.

In cases of interracial rape, the assailant is typically a stranger. This may be because casual social contact (e.g., having a drink in a bar), which often precedes rape, is frowned upon and thus less likely to occur when males and females are of different races. Since social norms tend to restrict the access of rapists to victims of different races, interracial rapes occur in settings where the victim is accessible and vulnerable. The victim may be seized in a park, on a street corner as she waits for a bus, while out shopping, or as she returns home from school or work. Very often a weapon is used to force her to submit. Many of these attacks thus occur in broad daylight as the woman, usually alone, performs the tasks which make up her daily routine. Consider the following scenario.

Jane, a black female, is in the midst of her daily three mile jog through the city. As she enters a residential area which adjoins her own neighborhood, she is suddenly knocked to the ground by a white assailant, a knife is placed to her throat and she is forced into a nearby alley. There she is raped and subjected to verbal threats and abuse. Afterward, she is released and manages to get to her home, where she tells her husband of the assault. What kinds of reactions might Jane have to the rape? The following are quite common:

1.   She might conclude that the rape was racially motivated. This is particularly likely in areas where considerable interracial tensions already exist or if verbal abuse from the rapist contained references to the victim's race.

2.   Since Jane is black and her assailant was white, she may have to spend additional time weighing the pros and cons of reporting the rape to the authorities. Often members of a racial minority lack confidence

in a legal system which they feel may not represent their interests.

3. Her anger towards the rapist may now generalize to all members of his race. As a result, rather than coming to grips with her feelings about this specific person, she "resolves" the incident by concluding that *all* white males (or black males, if the victim is white and the assailant is black) are rapists.

4. Related to the above, the victim may develop distrust and fear of all members of that race, experiencing anxiety and panic whenever they are in the general vicinity. Since daily activities often involve interracial contact, such reactions can be a serious impediment to her recovery.

5. Relationships with friends and acquaintances who are of the same race as the assailant may be affected adversely. Some women find themselves avoiding such acquaintances and therefore lose a portion of their social support system at a time when they most need it.

These kinds of reactions, especially ones which involve generalized anger towards all members of the assailant's race, are typical of those close to the victim as well. Keep in mind, however, that responses which focus on the assailant's race are counterproductive, since they distract the victim from the real issue, her feelings about *that particular person*. To help her respond to her victimization in a way which promotes a healthy resolution of the incident, there are several important points to keep in mind.

- Family and friends must be dissuaded from making racial slurs in the presence of the victim. Such comments may encourage her to attribute causality for the rape to the assailant's race, and thus keep her from coming to grips with her feelings toward the *individual* who assaulted her.

- You should remind her that not all male members of that race are rapists. If she has close friends or acquaintances of that race, point out to her that these individuals have been and will continue to be deserving of her trust and friendship. Also, as her recovery progresses, if you notice her avoiding contact with these acquaintances, you can perhaps suggest that she discuss this with her counselor, if she is seeing one.

- Reassure her that she did *not* put herself in a situation where rape could occur, that you do not hold her responsible for the assault, and that you in no way consider her to be "unclean" because she was raped by a member of another race.

- Since interracial rape so frequently occurs while the victim is in the midst of her daily activities, you must encourage her to resume those activities as soon as possible. Her attempts to prevent another assault by staying home from school, avoiding shopping trips, or simply refusing to venture out of the home will prevent her from reestablishing a sense of freedom and autonomy.

- Finally, you must deal with your own feelings about the incident, so that you can continue to provide your loved one with the affection and support she needs. In the case of interracial rape, it is quite natural for you to have difficulty in keeping your anger towards the rapist from generalizing to all members of his race. If so, contact a counselor or close friend and discuss your feelings with them.

Remember that even if the rape *appears* to be racially motivated, race is not the central issue in her victimization. The violence, injury and degradation that one human imposes upon another is the real tragedy of rape and should be the focus of your efforts to help her.

8
Reporting The Rape

Although it is a serious crime, rape frequently goes unreported. The reasons given by victims for not reporting rapes to the police include:

- a feeling that nothing can be done or it can't be proven that rape occurred;

- a feeling that rape is too personal for others to know about;

- an unwillingness to be "subjected" to the legal system; and

- a fear of reprisal.

In addition, for reasons discussed in this chapter, many reported rapes never go to trial. However, out of a desire that the rapist be punished or out of fear that he will attack others, an increasing number of women are willing to testify against their assailants. We believe that such a decision is especially

courageous given that a rape trial is both anxiety-producing
and psychologically exhausting for the woman. We believe
also that the decision whether or not to press charges should
be made *by the victim*, and that you should fully support her
decision, whatever it may be. In order to provide maximum
support for her, it is important that you understand the various
procedures initiated when the assault is reported (summarized
in a chart on the final page of this chapter) and the implica-
tions of her decision to pursue legal action.

The collection of evidence for a rape trial begins with a
preliminary police interview and a medical examination directly
following the rape episode. The sooner the police are notified,
the greater the likelihood of obtaining solid evidence that will
stand up in court. However, reporting to the police merely
gives the victim the option of later prosecution if she decides
to pursue the case. After she gives an initial report to uniformed
officers, perhaps at the emergency room, the victim must
undergo a medical examination to confirm that a sexual assault
has taken place. This exam, which is conducted *before* she
is allowed to bathe and change clothing, may entail a lengthy
wait in a hospital emergency room followed by a pelvic exam, test for venereal disease, vaginal, oral, and rectal swabs,
fingernail scrapings, and treatment for any injuries she may
have suffered. As you can well imagine, this kind of exam,
carried out by strangers in the immediate aftermath of a life-
threatening episode, is extremely unsettling to the woman. You
can help by being available to answer questions that might arise
and to ensure that medical personnel carry out their exam with
patience and sensitivity.

Shortly thereafter, perhaps the following day, a detective
will be assigned to the case. He or she will contact the victim
and arrange for her to give a statement at the police station.

In addition to giving and signing the statement, the victim may be asked to identify weapons or other evidence collected by the police, help construct a composite sketch of the assailant, and examine books of "mug" shots. Arrangements may also be made for her to take a polygraph exam to help verify her claim. Results of the polygraph exam can be used to help the police decide whether to prosecute the case, but are not admissible as evidence in a trial.

Rape victims do not always call the police immediately after the incident. Because you are loved and trusted by her, you may be the first person to whom she speaks about being raped. If this is the case, your immediate concern is to make certain she receives medical attention as soon as possible. There are two important reasons for an immediate medical examination. First, she may have suffered serious injuries other than obvious external cuts and bruises (e.g., internal bleeding). Second, medical evidence is crucial in establishing that a rape occurred; the longer the delay between the assault and the examination, the more difficult it is to secure this evidence.

In addition to ensuring that she receives proper medical care, being the first person to hear of her victimization has another important implication. If she reports the rape to the police, you very likely will be asked to provide them with your own statement in addition to hers. She may have told you details that she failed to recall when later questioned by the police. Furthermore, if the case goes to trial, you stand a good chance of serving as a witness on behalf of the state. If indeed you are placed in the position of having to endure lengthy questioning by police, the rape victim may feel an added responsibility for "dragging you into this situation." It is important for you to convey to her that your concern is for her well-being and that your assisting the police is only a minor inconvenience, especially if it means capturing the assailant.

Given the deeply personal and sensitive nature of rape evidence, being questioned by the police is usually emotionally draining for the victim. However, there are several strategies that may help reduce the emotional burden of recounting the episode to the police:

- She may request that you be present when she discusses the incident with investigators. Being with her at this moment can provide reassurance and make her feel less isolated. However, it is *very* important that you do not interrupt her account of events or interfere with police questioning. Despite your good intentions, it is not helpful for you to answer questions for her.

- She may request that you *not* be present during police questioning. Such reluctance to disclose to you the personal details of the rape during police interviews does not mean she is disregarding your feelings. It should be her decision to discuss the rape with you on her terms, at a time she feels is appropriate, without strangers being present. Respect her wishes in this matter and do not feel that she is slighting you.

- Many women feel more comfortable if a female police officer is present or actually conducting the questioning. If such a person is available, remind the victim to request her presence for the duration of the questioning.

- Most victims do not know what to expect when being questioned by police and are unclear as to why so many people are involved in obtaining information. Standard police procedures tend to create confusion for those not acquainted with these normal routines. Whenever possible, make sure that the police explain to the victim why they are proceeding in a particular fashion. Asking questions about what they do is not an implied criticism, but rather a way to reduce the understandable confusion she is experiencing.

- Because of the lengthy nature of most police interviews, she may have gone without food for a long period. If she is hungry, make sure that she is able to have a hot meal.

After questioning, the police will attempt to locate and arrest the suspect, if one has been identified. They will also contact the district attorney to discuss prosecution of the case. The police may advise against prosecution; that is, the rape complaint may be designated as "unfounded." Some reasons for "unfounding" a complaint are:

1. Delay in reporting by the victim

2. Previous victim-assailant relationship

3. Evidence that the victim was intoxicated or using illicit drugs

4. Refusal to undergo the medical examination

5. Failure to preserve relevant physical evidence (e.g., douching before reporting the crime)

6. "Victim precipitation" (e.g., hitchhiking, walking alone at night in a rough neighborhood, withdrawing from a previous agreement to have sexual relations)

7. Victim alters her story after filing charges

8. Circumstances associated with the incident are
    atypical or do not fit a "standard pattern" com-
    monly found by investigators, thus raising the suspi-
    cion that she is lying.

In addition to the reasons listed above, a victim may be
discouraged from filing charges if the police simply doubt her
credibility as a witness; that is, if her appearance and
"lifestyle" are such that the police and district attorney feel
her case would be difficult to prove in court. The police often
have a mental profile of whom they consider ideal or poor
witnesses. Such factors as "reputation," relationship to
assailant (e.g., ex-lover vs. total stranger) and whether or not
the victim abuses drugs or alcohol, influence how the police
will respond to the complaint. For example, the authors are
aware of a situation where two women were brutally raped
within several days of each other. In one case the victim was
a "go-go" dancer in a nightclub; the other was a college student. The police decided to pursue with vigor only the attack
against the student.

        You should be aware that the police and district attorney,
for a variety of reasons, may decide to prosecute the assailant
on some charge or charges other than rape. In fact, rape is
only one category under the broad heading of "sexual
assaults." These categories include: rape, sexual battery, cor-
ruption of a minor, gross sexual imposition, importuning,
voyeurism, and public indecency. Furthermore, the authorities
may decide to file charges on a number of other offenses which
seem incidental to the assault (e.g., breaking and entering,
burglary, aggravated robbery), if they feel there is strong
evidence to support them.

Filing charges sets in motion a lengthy and emotionally draining legal process wherein the truth and accuracy of the victim's story may repeatedly be called into question. Once the charges have been filed, the crime is viewed as an action against the state, with the woman simply serving as a witness on behalf of the state. The judicial system thus tends to depersonalize what is to the woman a singularly terrifying experience by emphasizing protection of "society," rather than the individual victim. Furthermore, what seems to the woman to be personal medical information now becomes part of the public record. (To the extent possible, you should work to preserve the woman's right to privacy by attempting to have her name withheld from newspaper accounts.) Shortly after charges are filed, the victim is usually asked to testify before a grand jury, which determines if there is enough evidence to indict the accused. (The accused and his attorney are *not* present at the grand jury proceedings.) If the victim fails to appear in court for this preliminary hearing, charges against the assailant may be dropped.

Once the victim completes this process, she may be called upon in the future to provide additional information. At some point, she should ask to see the police follow-up reports on her case. This is a useful means of ensuring that they accurately represented her position and have a complete account of the incident. Finally, you should inquire with the police or district attorney's office whether there is a victim restitution program in your community. Such programs can help to compensate victims for medical or other expenses incurred as a result of being raped.*

---

*For additional information on services for victims, contact Justice for Surviving Victims, P.O. Box 50248, Lighthouse Point, Florida 33064.

Keep in mind that this is an extremely trying time for the victim. She has by now recounted the incident to a number of *individuals*, but on this occasion she will be describing the details of the assault to a group of approximately 12 people (the grand jury, judge, district attorney, court reporter), almost all of whom are strangers. You can help her through this difficult time by reassuring her that her decision to pursue legal action is the proper one, by rehearsing her grand jury testimony with her, and by doing whatever you can to help her stay calm and composed as the time for her testimony approaches.

Reporting a Sexual Assault: Typical Procedures

The Immediate Aftermath

1. Reporting of incident to police

2. Initial police interview

3. Medical examination

The Next Day

4. Official statement given to police

5. Identification of weapons or other evidence collected by police

6. Identification of assailant (construction of composite sketch, examination of "mug shots")

7. Polygraph exam (not mandatory)

8. Charges filed

Apprehension of Suspect

9. Testimony before grand jury

10. Assailant indicted, trial date set (3 to 9 months after indictment)

9
The Trial

Once the assailant has been indicted, there is typically a three to nine month waiting period before the trial begins. This is a particularly difficult time for the woman for several reasons. First, her assailant may post bond and hence remain free to ''walk the streets.'' The woman is likely to experience an understandable fear that he will seek revenge. Also, family and friends of the rapist may call her and attempt to persuade or threaten her to drop the charges. Likewise, the defense attorney may attempt a number of delay tactics in the hope that she will not pursue the case. Perhaps most important of all, the woman is placed in a position of having to keep the incident in the forefront of her consciousness, remembering all of the details, until after the trial. In other words, during the pre-trial period she is given little opportunity to put the incident behind her and get on with her life.

The Pretrial Period

This pre-trial period requires great patience, understanding and support on your part. She may exhibit a number of

physiological and emotional patterns which you find distress-
ing (e.g., nightmares, insomnia, loss of appetite, fatigue,
depression, tension headaches, and generalized anxiety). It is
at this point that your relationship with her may undergo the
greatest stress. It is not uncommon for some men to feel annoyed at her for being ''too emotional'' and insist that she
cease talking and thinking about it. Some men develop a sense
of resentment toward the woman for having to spend increased
time with her or because she seems unresponsive to the man's
needs. Patience on your part is important at this time; it can
only add to the quality of your relationship in the long run.
We urge you to keep in mind two things.

1.   She did not choose this situation and feelings of
     anger and resentment on your part will only add
     to her distress.

2.   The difficult period she is going through is tem-
     porary and is likely to gradually diminish once the
     trial has ended.

A common experience among rape victims waiting for
the rape trial to begin is a considerable degree of apprehension about serving as a witness. Such anxiety is normal and
understandable when one considers the fact that many victims
have never even seen the inside of a courtroom, much less
having to speak into a microphone in front of a group of
strangers. Her anxiety may be compounded if there is poor
communication from the police and district attorney's office
concerning the dynamics of the legal process and what is expected of her as a witness. Furthermore, like most people she
may have only a vague idea of standard courtroom procedures,
the meaning of legal and medical jargon relevant to the case,
or proper courtroom decorum when testifying. Little wonder
if she has serious doubts about wanting to endure a trial.

To make matters worse, victims frequently come to feel that they are pawns in a legal chess game where they have no power to decide things which affect them directly. There are seemingly endless delays in finally bringing the case to trial. Typically the defense attorney will *deliberately* seek court delays as a tactic to discourage the victim. This is especially difficult for witnesses who must rearrange work schedules or travel from a long distance to testify. Likewise the district attorney may make some decisions about her case without consulting her. Furthermore, most of her contact with the police and district attorney's office will be at *their* convenience, not hers. In a very real sense, the impersonal character of the legal system can function to dehumanize the rape victim and further strain her emotional resources.

In order to help her regain a sense of control and prepare her for what to expect in court, there are a number of things you can do. Although no two cases are exactly alike, the following suggestions are of use in preparing her for trial.

- Encourage her to request from the district attorney a copy of her signed statement given to the police shortly after the incident. This statement is important evidence and reviewing it will refresh her memory of the event. If there are discrepancies between this statement and subsequent courtroom testimony, the defense attorney may claim she is an unreliable witness in an attempt to discredit her. It is very important that she remember the detailed sequence of events to avoid appearing confused on the witness stand. Preparing for trial is like preparing for an exam and studying her earlier statement is an important way to avoid inconsistencies in the testimony.

• Another way to help her recall significant details is by accompanying her to the scene of the crime, *if she agrees*. Because of the potentially disturbing nature of such a visit, she alone should make this decision. However, visiting the physical location will help her describe it in court and may stimulate her recollection in other important ways. In addition, a visit to the crime scene may occur in the process of the trial anyway; if so, a prior visit with you will better prepare her for it.

• To familiarize her with the setting, accompany her to the courtroom several days in advance of the trial. Pay special attention to the position of the witness stand and the direction she will face when giving testimony. If possible, it may be that you or a trusted family member could sit in public seating located directly in her line of vision from the witness stand. If she has a sympathetic face to look upon while testifying, rather than the defense attorney or assailant, it may help to ease her tension.

• Help her to mentally rehearse being a witness by asking her questions about the ''alleged incident'' just as a defense attorney would do. To the extent that she can imagine what the trial may entail, she may feel more comfortable about testifying. If at all possible and *if* she is willing, attending other rape trials is an excellent way to be prepared. Likewise, many rape crisis centers can provide legal counseling to victims to help them prepare for court.

• Because she has to describe in detail what transpired during the rape, she needs to be comfortable with

THE TRIAL   57

"appropriate" terminology to describe sex acts. Make sure she is familiar with terms such as fellatio, sodomy and cunnilingus. This will help her avoid the use of "slang" terms which may discredit her.

- Double check with friends or other witnesses who have been subpoenaed to testify at the trial. Make sure they are aware of the correct time and location of the trial, and if necessary, help them arrange transportation or baby sitting.

- If the defense attorney asks to talk to her, she is under no obligation to do so and may refuse. Likewise, if she or those close to her receive threatening communications from the family or friends of the rapists, the district attorney should be informed.

- Finally, make sure she is mentally prepared for the possibility of last minute delays or for a plea bargain before the case goes to trial. If it is clear that the victim is determined to stick with the case despite various delay tactics, many assailants will plead guilty to a lesser charge (e.g., attempted rape) in order to avoid the possibility of a longer sentence. Although the decision to accept a plea of guilty to reduced charges is made by the district attorney without necessarily consulting the victim, at least it has the benefit of sparing her the ordeal of a trial.

Most women find the rape trial to be a negative experience, though for some it is therapeutic. Usually the most difficult aspect of the trial is the fact that the woman is called upon to publicly testify. This means that she must reveal the details

of her rape to a group of strangers and be subject to cross examination by an attorney who will attempt to attack her
character and question her version of events. Frequently the
defense attorney will ask leading questions that imply a history
of sexual promiscuity. Many victims are made to feel that it
is they who are on trial, not the assailant. Finally, the trial
itself is usually the first time the victim must confront her
assailant face-to-face. In a very real sense, she is alone in front
of a crowd, speaking publicly of a deeply private and
humiliating experience. Without the support and understanding of you and others close to her, the courtroom experience
threatens to further traumatize the rape victim and undermine
her feeling of self-reliance.

Giving Testimony

During the trial, the defense attorney is likely to defend
the rapist using one of three arguments.

1.   The rape never took place and the story was in-
     vented by the woman in order to seek revenge or
     simply call attention to herself.

2.   The rape did take place but the defendant was
     mistakenly identified as the assailant.

3.   The woman was not a victim of rape but a willing
     participant in sexual intercourse.

Regardless of the approach taken by the defense, the victim
usually has her character and judgment called into question

during the cross-examination. The defense attorney may claim that she was too hysterical to make positive identification; that she fabricated events to "get even" or because she wants others to think she is sexually attractive; that she is sexually promiscuous and would have intercourse with anyone; that she somehow precipitated the event or otherwise assumed the risk and is therefore responsible; or any other argument that undermines her credibility as a witness. Remember that the role of the defense attorney is to create doubt in the minds of judge and jury, so both she and you should be prepared to encounter accusations about her character and stereotypes about how women should act in various situations.

In order to prepare her to present testimony (or prepare you if you are a witness), there are several points to keep in mind.

- To the extent possible, answer all questions directly without appearing uncertain. Statements such as "I don't know" or "I'm not sure" tend to raise doubts among the judge and jury.

- Be prepared for interruptions while giving testimony. People may wander in and out of court or the attorney may request a recess even though the testimony is in progress.

- While testifying, it is helpful to speak in a clear and deliberate manner. Take your time before responding to questions and maintain eye contact with others in the room rather than staring at the floor.

- Being properly dressed and well-groomed enhances the credibility of the witness. Do not wear blue jeans, shorts, T-shirt or tennis shoes to the courtroom. Do not chew gum; the judge or jury might find it distracting.

After the Trial

Despite the difficulties of a rape trial, hopefully there
is an important consolation—the conviction of the victim's
assailant. At the very least, the trial provides the victim with
an opportunity to express her anger toward the rapist and feel
a degree of justice being served. During and after the trial,
it is important that you convey to her that she is not "changed"
in your eyes and in no way should she feel guilty for what
happened in the courtroom. Because cross-examination tends
to promote feelings of self-doubt, inadequacy and confusion,
it is especially important that you reassure her of your continued
faith in her judgment and character. Many victims emerge from
a rape trial with anger and resentment toward a legal system
that seems to "protect the criminal and condemn the victim."
A heightened sensitivity on your part to the difficulties of a
rape trial is a great asset in maintaining a positive relationship with her and helping her deal with these feelings.

Given the nature of rape cases, there is a distinct possibility
that the offender will go free. If this is the situation, under
no circumstances should you or others close to the victim
attempt to take justice into your own hands. Rather, there is
one other legal avenue that the victim can pursue. Although
most victims are not aware of this option, she has the right
to sue the rapist for damages. Such action would be a *civil*
case rather than a criminal one. This would require her to retain
a lawyer and absorb all legal fees. She should be informed
of this option but it should be *her* decision as to whether her
financial and emotional resources are sufficient to continue
the legal process.

Once legal action has been completed, it may be helpful
to discuss with the victim the likelihood of future contacts with

the rapist. Working together to determine ways of coping with and/or avoiding such encounters may help reduce anxiety. In addition, you must both be aware that the successful completion of legal action will not "make everything right." For one thing, if the rapist appeals the conviction, it may result in a second trial which again requires her to be a witness.

Much of the fear, anger and hurt could continue to persist after the trial. She may even feel responsible for the fact that a man was sent to prison, even though he was found guilty. Simply remind her that the judge and jury determined his fate, not she. Moreover, many rapists have committed *multiple* offenses and her courageousness in going to trial may have saved others from a similar ordeal. Finally, individual counseling for her and relationship counseling for the two of you may be helpful in bringing about some resolution of intense feelings, thus enabling you both to get on with your lives.

10
Protecting Against Rape

Once a woman has been raped, it is common for her to experience prolonged and deep-seated fears concerning her safety. Unless one has had the experience of being the victim of criminal assault, it is often difficult to understand why others who have been victims appear to be preoccupied with personal safety. Given the suddenness and extreme violence of rape, it is understandable for victims to feel an enduring sense of uneasiness or tension about everyday events that others take for granted. Fear of strangers, fear of going out of the house, and fear of being alone are just a few examples that are common to women who have been raped. It is important for you to realize that fears concerning personal safety, although seemingly "silly" or "unreasonable" from an outsider's standpoint, are rational and understandable from the victim's point of view. Furthermore, her state of mind is not likely to change simply because family or friends tell her that her fears are "ridiculous."

Personal Protection

While it is true that there is no foolproof means to prevent future assaults, there are some steps to be taken which may ease a rape victim's fears and enhance her safety. The following represents a list of do's and don'ts which both you and she can take into account as a means of avoiding rape situations. This list has been compiled from a variety of lists suggesting protective measures against rape.

- Make sure her home is safe with deadbolt locks on doors, peep-hole viewer and window locks. Change the locks when moving to a new residence.

- If a stranger should come to the door, do not allow him in or indicate that no one else is home. Ask delivery or service persons for identification and do not allow children to ask strangers into the house. Make phone calls for strangers when there is an emergency. If a woman is alone in the house, she should pretend there is someone else home when a stranger visits.

- Women living alone should not list the first name on mail boxes or in telephone directories. In apartment complexes, women should avoid remaining alone in laundry rooms, basements, or garages. Make sure the entrance to the house is well-lighted.

- Always keep car doors locked, including when driving, and park in lighted areas. Before getting into a car, check the back seat. If there is car trouble, open the hood, attach a white cloth to the door and remain inside the locked car. If followed in a car by a stranger, drive directly to the police station.

- If one cannot avoid being alone on the street or a college campus late at night, stay in the areas which are lighted and carry a police whistle. Never hitchhike!

- In the context of dating, be clear as to boundaries of acceptable sexual activity before any "misunderstandings" occur.

Although there is considerable debate as to whether active resistance to an attack will help or further endanger the victim, some claim that proficiency in self-defense techniques can provide an additional measure of safety. Others suggest that passive resistance, ranging from gentle persuasion to acting hysterically, may dissuade an assailant. The simple fact is that no one can say what is *always* the best response to an attack. Characteristics of the assailant and the circumstances will vary. All one can say is that anything which helps the victim to survive an attack is the right thing to do.

Involvement With The Community

As we have indicated throughout this book, the experience of having a loved one endure the trauma of rape is likely to elicit powerful emotions in you: anger, sympathy, frustration, shame, grief and futility, to mention a few. While such feelings are understandable, we have emphasized that your primary concern should be directed toward the recovery of the woman. Do not hesitate to take advantage of agency services available in your community which offer counseling for rape victims and their loved ones.

It is possible for you to "work through" some of your feelings, especially feelings of futility, by taking constructive action to help both actual and potential rape victims. Working as a volunteer with various citizen action groups can channel your energies in a positive manner. Specifically, you can assist other rape victims and help to reduce the incidence of rape by serving as a volunteer in the following areas:

- Helping with counseling and support services for rape victims (e.g., working the 24 hour crisis hotline)

- Raising public consciousness about rape (e.g., distributing rape-related literature, helping sponsor community forums and workshops on rape, etc.)

- Working to bring about legal reform and changes in the criminal justice system (e.g., writing letters to state representatives concerning rape legislation, examining police and medical procedures for rape victims, etc.)

In many communities, rape crisis centers have been established and are already working in these and related areas. Serving as a volunteer in one of these agencies can be both a constructive outlet for your feelings and provide a badly needed service to others. At the very least, you may wish to contact the organizations listed below and ask for further information about how you can become involved.

National Resources

National Center for the Prevention and Control of Rape
Room 15-99, Parklawn Building
5600 Fishers Lane
Rockville, MD 20857

National Coalition Against Sexual Assault (NCASA)*
P.O. Box 7156
Austin, TX 78712
(512) 472-7273

National Board YWCA of the U.S.A.
600 Lexington Avenue
New York, NY 10022
(212) 753-4700

Local Resources

There are many ways to locate such resources in your community:
1.   Check the telephone directory.

2.   Call your local hospital or police department.

3.   Check with other human service agencies such as Child Guidance, Child Protective Services, or the YWCA. If there are rape crisis services in your area, they will be aware of them.

4.   In the event all the above attempts fail, contact one of the national organizations listed above. Staff members will be able to help you find the closest possible rape crisis service in your area.

---

*At the time of this printing, NCASA is working toward having a national office. However, it currently establishes its headquarters on a rotating basis with the individual serving a two year term as its president. The Austin Rape Crisis Center has kindly allowed us to list that agency where the current president is located and will provide the correct NCASA address and phone number as it changes in the future.

11
A Final Note

We wish to stress once again that *you* can play a major role in helping a loved one recover from rape. However, there are no "miracle cures" and it is not likely that you alone can immediately "make everything right." By realizing that through sympathetic understanding you will exert a positive but necessarily limited influence, you can avoid the tendency to take personal responsibility for another person's "ultimate happiness." By being patient, supportive, and non-judgmental toward her you will be communicating the most important message—your unconditional love. Finally, trust that she is strong enough to do the rest on her own.

Appendix A
Illustrative Case Studies*

While there are many possible reactions to the rape of a loved one, the following case studies which we have selected will help you to do what is right. These case studies are representative of many of the things one should and should not do when dealing with a rape victim. The most important point to remember is that the husbands, fathers and male friends of rape victims can be helpful or they can be harmful. With patience and understanding, men can minimize the terror and degradation experienced by women who have been raped.

Case Study 1
Wendy: A Teenage Victim

The Incident

Wendy, a 14 year old girl, was spending a few days with her girlfriend Betsy and Betsy's family at their summer cottage. One afternoon Wendy and Mark, Betsy's 16 year old brother, paddled the canoe to the far end of the lake—a heavily wooded area where there were no other cottages. Mark told Wendy that he had a bottle of wine and asked her if she would like to sit on the bank and drink with him. Always a rather adventuresome child, Wendy agreed to Mark's suggestion.

*Despite alterations, the names and situations in these illustrative case studies are substantively accurate and represent real experiences.

Although Mark drank the lion's share of wine, Wendy had a sufficient amount to feel light-headed and rather silly. Perhaps mistaking her elevated spirits as an indication of flirtatiousness, Mark put his arm around Wendy and began to kiss her on the lips. This was the first time Wendy had ever been kissed and, being rather taken back, she literally did not know how to respond. What's more, Mark did not stop at that point but aggressively began petting her. This frightened Wendy, but her inexperience in these matters caused her to be passive and not say anything. Suddenly Mark removed his bathing suit and told Wendy to do likewise. Frightened and confused, Wendy said she wanted to go back to the cottage. With a forceful tone, Mark said everything would be "all right" and that there was nothing for her to fear. In a rapid series of moves, he pulled off the bottom of Wendy's suit, pushed her on her back and entered her. In a state of shock, fear, confusion and physical pain, Wendy could only cry.

Although the entire episode lasted only a few minutes, Wendy continued to cry for a long time. Her emotional state began to frighten Mark. Through her tears, Wendy managed to say "Why did you do that? You shouldn't have done that to me!" Mark clearly was scared. He tried to console her by indicating that it was only normal for people who liked each other to "make love." Then he said, "Besides, you should have said something earlier if you really didn't want to."

After returning to the cottage Wendy said nothing to Betsy or to the parents. In fact, Wendy said nothing to her own parents after she returned home. However, her emotional state and her behavior were definitely altered. Wendy was not clear as to her responsibility in the matter. She was certain that her parents would be angry with her if they knew she had been drinking. Even though her parents noticed that Wendy appeared to be moody and uncommunicative, they assumed it was merely a "phase."

Shortly after the new school year began, Wendy became ill at school for several consecutive days. Upon recommendation from the school nurse, Wendy received a medical exam which revealed that she was pregnant. Neither she nor her parents had suspected her condition.

Others React

The revelation of Wendy's pregnancy produced extreme anger in her parents, particularly her father. He could barely contain himself as he screamed his demands that she explain herself. Because Wendy had never communicated about sexual matters with her parents, she found it extremely difficult to discuss the event, especially with her father. Her understandable reluctance only served to escalate his anger to a point where he threatened to kick her out of the house. Finally, she broke down in fits of weeping and managed to describe what had happened.

Wendy gave an honest account to her parents, though her inexperience in the area of sexuality deeply embarrassed her and compounded her difficulties in communicating. Wendy had many unanswered questions in her own mind, but the anger of her parents made it difficult for her to share those questions and receive feedback. She had questions about her own sexuality, about the nature of pregnancy, about whether others blamed her, and about what would happen to her friendship with Betsy and other peers. In addition, Wendy had great concern over what should be done with the baby and whether or not she would be able to finish school. The anger and shame of her parents only added to the depression Wendy was feeling.

Without asking Wendy's opinion, her parents decided to send her away to a special school for the duration of her pregnancy. When the child was born, it would be placed for adoption without Wendy ever seeing it. In addition, her father sought legal action against Mark and his parents on a wide variety of charges. Again, this action was taken without consulting Wendy. Furthermore, Wendy was denied the right to see her group of friends. Her every move was carefully scrutinized by her father. Finally, Wendy's entire family engaged in a "conspiracy of silence" wherein her "encounter" (they avoided using the word rape) and subsequent condition were never mentioned by anyone.

Although Wendy's parents meant well, her feelings about what was happening seemed to be of secondary importance to the feelings and wishes of her mother and father. It was clear that her parents, especially her father—whose will usually prevailed in family matters—were embarrassed by the situation. They tended to blame Wendy for poor judgment. Even though Wendy received proper medical attention, her parents never sought to provide her with counseling. In a state of utter depression, feeling isolated, insecure and guilty, Wendy attempted to take her life. Although she survived the attempt, her physical and mental state were such that she had to be hospitalized for a lengthy period of time.

In the spring, Wendy gave birth to a baby girl whom she never saw. Although that was several years ago, the impact of those events is still very much evident in her life. Wendy has continued to receive professional help but her emotional recovery has been slow and very painful.

Lessons To Be Learned

In a sense, Wendy became a multiple victim of a single crime. She was victimized not only by rape, but also by an unwanted pregnancy and a lack of understanding in the home. Unfortunately, her situation is similar to that of many teenagers who have been raped.

In almost every instance, the reactions of her parents, especially her father, compounded Wendy's emotional trauma; they made matters worse. Rather than communicating unconditional love and support, Wendy's parents communicated anger and embarrassment.

When Wendy's parents learned of her rape and pregnancy, a calm and understanding approach was in order. The anger and threats of her parents made it difficult for Wendy to express her feelings. She was being blamed for poor judgment and lack of character when in fact, her only "fault" was a lack of understanding and experience in sexual matters. Unfortunately, Wendy was never provided with an appropriate resource person with whom she could have frank discussions about sexuality and pregnancy. In the absence of information, Wendy's fears continued to grow.

At every phase in the decision making process, Wendy should have been given the opportunity to share her feelings. Decisions affecting her should not have been made without her input. This is especially true in respect to the decisions made for her about her schooling and her baby.

Wendy's parents also made the mistake of isolating her from her network of friends at a time when she most needed them. Limiting contact with her peers (including her friend, Betsy) reflected her parents' shame rather than an awareness of Wendy's needs. Finally, the "conspiracy of silence" prevailing in the home communicated to Wendy that her behavior was too awful to even be discussed. Feeling guilty, confused, isolated and unable to communicate with those persons she loved most, it is not surprising that Wendy's depression led to an attempted suicide.

What Wendy's Parents Should Have Done

- **Wendy's parents should have responded to her need for unconditional love.** Parents who spend time blaming others or themselves for the rape of their child waste valuable time and energy. This energy should be directed toward reassuring and supporting the victim.

- **Wendy's parents should have let her know that someone would be willing to talk to her about adult intimacy.** Since the rape was Wendy's first sexual experience, Wendy needed reassurance that her fears and questions about adult intimacy could be discussed. Such a discussion with either her parents, a trusted adult, or a counselor, would have helped Wendy realize that her capacity for sexual intimacy in adulthood had not been diminished.

- **Wendy's parents should have arranged for professional assistance to help the family communicate more effectively.** Unfortunately, counseling to help Wendy deal with the rape, her pregnancy, and her parents' reactions was not provided until after Wendy's attempted suicide. Early professional assistance would have improved the communication between Wendy and her parents. Communication between parents and adolescents is often strained even under normal conditions. During the crisis produced by rape, effective communication is made even more difficult. Improved communication paired with greater understanding and support at home would have spared Wendy and her family a great deal of unnecessary pain and would have greatly helped her in her recovery.

• **Wendy's parents should have allowed Wendy to return to her normal activities.** By encouraging Wendy to resume her normal lifestyle as much as possible, her parents would have provided her with a much needed sense of normalcy. It also would have increased Wendy's access to her friends and peers who could have provided important support in times of trouble.

• **Wendy's parents should have been more considerate of her rights and feelings.** Such consideration would have helped Wendy to not feel punished and excluded. When Wendy's parents refused to discuss with Wendy the rape experience and Wendy's future, they communicated that they were ashamed of her; that they held her responsible for her own rape. Had Wendy's parents listened to her and included her in the decision making process, she would not have felt so isolated and could have taken an active role in her recovery process.

Case Study 2

Carla: A Case of Acquaintance Rape

The Incident

Carla is 28 years old, single and teaches elementary school in a suburban community. While returning to her apartment from a dance class one evening, she was approached in the parking lot by her former boyfriend, Ron. Even though they had stopped dating—by mutual agreement—nearly a year ago, Ron still called her from time to time. Carla sensed that he had never totally accepted the fact that their relationship was over. On this occasion Ron seemed distraught. Even though she could smell alcohol on his breath, Carla agreed to let him come inside and talk about what was troubling him.

Once they were inside her apartment, there was an abrupt change in Ron's mood. He became very belligerent and aggressive. He told Carla that even though she was now dating another man, she would always be his girl. Carla could tell by now that Ron had been drinking heavily. She became concerned for her safety. She recalled two occasions during their dating relationship when Ron was physically abusive to her after he had been drinking. She tried to calm him down and offered to make coffee, but Ron was too drunk and angry to listen to reason. He told her that he thought it would be the "right thing" for them to make love. Carla strongly refused. He then slapped her and forced her into the bedroom where he raped her. Afterwards, he warned her not to say anything to anyone and joked that even if she did, no one would believe her anyway.

As soon as he left, Carla composed herself somewhat and tried to decide what to do. Should she report the rape to the police? If she did report it, would the police believe her? After nearly an hour of soul-searching, she decided to call her boyfriend, Dale. She was confident that Dale would believe her and would help her decide on the right course of action.

Others React

Dale arrived within 15 minutes and Carla, though considerably upset, told him what had happened. Dale was shocked and confused by her story. He wanted to ask her what she was doing with Ron in the first place and why he was in her apartment. However, he realized that Carla needed support and advice, not questions. Although Dale said it was her decision, he advised her to report the assault to the police. Even though the police might question a charge of rape against a former boyfriend, Dale felt that Carla would have to bring charges against Ron or run the risk of being raped again. Carla agreed. Within two days, Ron was arrested and charged with rape. Shortly thereafter, he was indicted at a preliminary hearing and a trial date was set.

Meanwhile, Carla returned to work after a week's leave of absence. She and Dale tried to resume their normal pattern of social activities. Privately, though, Dale was having doubts. Carla had told him several times that her relationship with Ron was over. However, she had said also that Ron called her occasionally to "talk about old times." In addition, a mutual friend of Ron and Carla's told Dale that she had known Ron for several years and found it difficult to believe he would force himself on Carla. Ron, for his part, was strongly denying that he had raped Carla, even though he admitted to having sexual relations with her that night. After all, he reasoned, they had virtually lived together at one time and had continued to maintain regular contact with one another.

Dale felt guilty for doubting Carla's version of events, but the doubts would not go away. At the same time, they stopped socializing with many of their friends because a number of them were also friends of Ron. Several mutual friends had hinted that Carla probably agreed to have sexual relations with Ron, later calling it rape to preserve her relationship with Dale. As the strain on their relationship grew, Carla and Dale argued more frequently and were no longer able to communicate openly with each other. Finally, Dale confronted her with his suspicions that she had fabricated the rape charge to cover up her own promiscuity. Carla wanted to prove to Dale that his suspicions were unfounded. However, his unwillingness to trust and support her convinced her that it was not worth the effort. She thus became increasingly isolated from Dale and her friends.

To make matters worse, the district attorney decided that there was not sufficient evidence to yield a conviction. As a result, the case was dropped. In Dale's mind, this confirmed his worst suspicions about Carla's fidelity and honesty. No longer able to effectively communicate, Dale and Carla ended their relationship. Since then Carla has lost contact with a number of her former friends and has found it increasingly difficult to resume dating other men.

Lessons To Be Learned

The impact of Carla's rape on her relationship with her male friend, Dale, is similar to that of many other cases of acquaintance rape. Initially, Dale appeared supportive and understanding. He did not pressure Carla with questions but rather attempted to do what was best for Carla. However, Dale's ability to be supportive gradually eroded in the face of his doubts about her honesty and fidelity. In attending to the comments of their mutual friends, Dale allowed casual gossip to cloud his trust of Carla. He therefore jeopardized their ability to communicate. Dale could have been more helpful to Carla and himself if he had approached the situation differently.

What Dale Should Have Done

- **Dale should have applauded Carla's willingness to help a friend in distress (even if that friend was a former lover).** Instead of communicating doubts about her honesty, he would have demonstrated his trust in Carla and their love for each other. Had Dale realized the trust Carla had placed in him by confiding in him, he may not have doubted her fidelity.

- **Dale should have considered professional counseling.** A professional counselor could have helped Dale realize that the expression of friendship which Carla extended to Ron did not imply any desire for sexual intimacy. Through counseling, Dale would have learned to reassure Carla that she was in no way responsible for Ron's sexual assault upon her.

Case Study 3

Lisa: Rape Victim With Nonsupportive Partner

The Incident

At approximately 3:00 a.m. on a hot summer night, Lisa was awakened from a sound sleep by the presence of someone in her bedroom. At first she thought it was her four year old son Tommy, but an instant later she was frozen in terror when the figure of a man hovered over her and said, "Bitch, I'm gonna rape you; if you scream, I'll go after your kid." Lisa's terror was so complete that she could neither speak nor move. She was engulfed in a sensation of "unreality," almost as if she were watching a movie rather than being the victim of a horrifying event. As the man began to remove her bed clothing, Lisa's immediate concern was for the safety of her son and so she did not fight her assailant.

As the stranger descended upon her, Lisa managed to say, "Please! Please don't!" In a half mocking, half vengeful voice the man replied, "I've been watching you and I think you're gonna like this." Reeking of alcohol and whispering profanities in her ear, the man proceeded to rape her. The room was dark and Lisa never saw his face. After ten minutes, which seemed like an eternity, the stranger started to leave. He turned back to Lisa, "If you try calling the police, I'll be back. This is between you and me—if I have to come back, you and your kid won't be so lucky next time." With those words, the rapist bolted through an open window into the night. Lisa ran into Tommy's room, saw that he was undisturbed, and then sat down trembling and weeping.

Lisa did not go to the police. She did not speak of the incident to anyone. Rather, she waited for her husband Barry, who would return in two weeks from his current tour of duty in the Navy. Those two weeks were filled with fear for herself and her son. She had a great deal of self-doubt as to whether she had done the right thing, as well as considerable apprehension over how her husband would respond. For some time their marriage had been on shaky ground. Lisa knew that her rape was going to complicate an already stressful situation.

Others React

When her husband Barry finally returned home, he sensed almost immediately that Lisa was behaving in an unusual way. He asked her what was wrong. Not wanting to spoil Barry's homecoming, she claimed that everything was fine. However, her expression betrayed her words. Barry, never a particularly patient man, began to lose his temper and insisted that she tell him about the problem. Lisa could contain her tears no longer and blurted out that she had been raped.

Barry sat in stunned silence as Lisa recounted the event. He did not interrupt her but he clearly was becoming angry. When she finished, he said, "If I catch the b . . . . . . , I'm going to kill him!" He told her that she shouldn't worry because he'd find a way to "get" the guy. He then proceeded to ask Lisa for information that would help him identify the rapist. "What did he look like?" "How tall was he?" "How old did he seem?" "What was he wearing?" "What did his voice sound like?" When Lisa claimed that she had no idea who the man was and appeared unable to provide Barry with answers, he became very annoyed with her and implied that she was being uncooperative. He never asked if she had seen a doctor or if she needed someone to talk to about the incident.

During the next several days, Barry appeared to be preoccupied with the rape and talked of it constantly. Not only was he deeply angered, he was also beginning to have doubts about Lisa's role in her victimization. He began to ask her questions such as, "Why didn't you lock the window?" "Why didn't you fight him?" "What do you think you did to make him pick you?" "Why did you decide not to call the police?" "Are you sure you don't have any idea who the guy is?" Even though this type of questioning upset Lisa very much, her husband seemed unable to contain his anger or doubts. He continued to make her discuss the incident.

Other aspects of their relationship also suffered. Barry spent little time with their son, preferring instead to be at the tavern "thinking." In terms of their sexual relationship, Lisa was confused and upset by what happened to her; she simply could not respond to Barry's advances. At first he appeared to be understanding and did not force the issue. Then one night after he had been drinking, Barry insisted that she "stop acting like a child and start acting like a wife." When Lisa apologized but still remained reluctant, Barry became abusive. He pushed her down and screamed at her, "If you can do it with him, you can do it with me!" Never did Lisa feel more alone than at that moment.

Barry was home for approximately six weeks before his next tour of duty. All the problems that existed in their marriage before Lisa's rape were exaggerated and brought out into the open. By the end of his stay, it was apparent that their marriage was in serious trouble. Lisa became aware of a fundamental failure in communication. She felt that Barry had abandoned her emotionally when she most needed him. For his part, the rape enhanced Barry's suspicions about Lisa's faithfulness. He could not understand why she seemed so cold and distant.

In a way, the anger that each felt toward the rapist shifted toward the other person.

After Barry departed, Lisa and her son moved back to her parent's house. She is currently seeking the assistance of a counselor and is undecided about whether she is committed to continuing her marriage with Barry.

Lessons To Be Learned

It is clear from Lisa's case that her husband's anger and distrust blinded Barry to her condition and the problems she was facing. His initial preoccupation with revenge and his doubts about Lisa's judgment and fidelity only heightened her distress. Barry's drinking, his anger toward Lisa, and his premature demands that she be sexually responsive to his needs put severe strains upon their relationship. This prolonged her recovery. It also reduced Barry's ability to function as a father, husband and lover. If Barry was to have played a positive role in Lisa's recovery, he should have acted much differently.

What Barry Should Have Done

- **Barry's first concern should have been Lisa's physical and mental welfare**. Barry should have insisted that his wife undergo a thorough medical examination. Not only would this have protected Lisa from disease and physical harm which may have resulted from the rape, it would also have been a demonstration of his love and support.

- **Barry should have put his feelings aside, listened carefully to Lisa and taken his cues from her**. Barry's quick interest in revenge was an indication that he was much more concerned with his own feelings than with those of his wife.

- **Barry should have refrained from "interrogating" Lisa**. In so doing, he would have greatly reduced her feelings of guilt and anxiety. Words of comfort and support were needed to assure Lisa that she was a victim; she was not in any way to blame for the rape.

- **Barry should have encouraged Lisa to seek the assistance of a counselor, perhaps at the nearest rape crisis center. He should have also considered relationship counseling.** Their marriage, which was in some jeopardy prior to the rape, was now in serious trouble. With professional help, communications between Barry and Lisa could have been improved.

- **Barry should not have intimidated Lisa into having sexual relations with him.** By so doing, Barry demonstrated a lack of understanding and respect for the pain and terror Lisa experienced. His actions toward her communicated that he considered her to be a willing participant in a sexual act with a stranger—not a victim of violence. Barry should have known that a woman who has been raped requires time to recover. She needs time to regain her normal desire for sexual intimacy. He should have been with Lisa to hold and comfort her—not to make sexual demands.

- **Barry should not have "abandoned" Lisa and their son.** In failing to spend time with his son,

Barry placed the full responsibility of child care on Lisa. Her recovery would have been much easier if he had freed her from some of her daily responsibilities. In addition, his absence from the home not only caused Lisa to worry, but also communicated his rejection of her and their son.

Case Study 4

Barbara: Rape Complicated by Racial Prejudice

The Incident

Barbara is a white, 45 year old housewife who resides in a large city on the east coast. She and her husband Paul, a bus driver for the city transit system, have three children. Barbara does her grocery shopping every Tuesday morning at the same local supermarket where she has shopped for 13 years.

On this particular Tuesday, Barbara left the store with two armloads of groceries and walked around the side of the building to her automobile. As she reached her car, two black men in their early twenties approached her and offered to help put the groceries in the trunk. Before she could reply, one of the men pulled out a knife and placed it to her throat while the other clamped a hand over her mouth and spun her around by the arm. As the groceries scattered in all directions, Barbara was dragged behind a dumpster and gagged with her own scarf. It was broad daylight and she could see houses across the street, but there were no people in sight. She was raped repeatedly by the two men and subjected to a stream of verbal abuse which left little doubt as to how the two men felt about white females.

When the ordeal was finally over, the two rapists seemed surprisingly remorseful and were almost considerate. They helped her to her feet, brushed the dirt off her clothes, picked up the groceries on the ground beside her car and tossed them into the back seat. As soon as she was inside the car, she locked the doors and drove directly home. Once inside the garage, she began weeping.

Others React

She was still crying 15 minutes later when her youngest son Tim, age 15, arrived home from school. He wanted to know what had happened. She simply told him to call the dispatcher at the transit company to request that her husband Paul be sent straight home. By the time Paul arrived, their daughter Karen, age 17, had also returned home from school. Barbara sent the children out of the room while she told the story to her husband. Paul called the police, who suggested that he take Barbara to the hospital immediately for an examination. Two uniformed officers met them there to take a preliminary statement from Barbara.

Before leaving for the hospital Paul told the children: "Your mother has been raped by two black men. She's going to be all right, but she needs some medical attention. Then she has to talk to the police. I'll call you from the hospital. In the meantime, call your older brother at work and tell him what's happened." With that, Paul and Barbara left for the hospital.

Blake, the eldest son, left work at the foundry when his brother called. He drove to his parent's house to await the call from his father. As might be expected, Blake's younger siblings looked to him for guidance. When his father called home to recount what had happened, Blake went into an angry tirade about black people and "other low lifes who should be shot." He was convinced that the police and courts would probably do nothing about the crime and that the only way to guarantee justice was to "take it into your own hands."

For weeks after the rape, there seemed to be little progress in apprehending the rapists. Both Paul and Blake continually discussed, in front of the rest of the family, their feelings about black people who "live off the sweat of others, commit all the crimes, and still go free." These frequent expressions of outrage were beginning to have a profound impact on the others. For example, Karen became very reluctant to talk to one of her fellow high school cheerleaders who was black. She also felt very uneasy about black males at school, even though she had been on good terms with them all during high school.

Tim was also influenced by the racial sentiments of his father and older brother. He began to notice things about the blacks at school that had never before drawn his attention. He avoided sitting near blacks on the school bus and in the cafeteria. He and his friends found themselves frequently discussing how black people were "different" and how they always seemed to be the trouble makers at school. One day Tim and his friends vandalized several lockers used by black students. This in turn heightened racial tensions at school and set off several other interracial incidents. Tim and the others were caught and had to pay for damages. They also spent considerable time in detention. Although Tim's actions were frowned upon by school officials, at home his father and brother treated him like a hero.

As a consequence, Barbara was deeply affected not only by her victimization but also by the perpetual discussions about blacks. Instead of the tension in the home subsiding during the weeks following the rape, it grew worse. Barbara became increasingly fearful that members of her family would end up hurt or in jail. She was especially upset over what happened to Tim at school. When she discovered that Blake had purchased a gun and was keeping it in his car, she was at a total loss as to what she could do. Finally, in order to protect Blake from himself she removed the weapon from his car and threw it in the river. This made both her husband and Blake angry with her. The rapists were never caught but the subject of race continues to be an issue of contention in Barbara's family.

Lessons To Be Learned

Due to her family's preoccupation with "racial justice," Barbara's needs and victimization were poorly attended. Barbara's need for emotional support was shoved aside because of emotionally charged racial prejudices. As a result, the family became divided rather than united. Under no circumstances should Paul and Blake have been angry with Barbara for her actions concerning the gun. They needed to realize that her motive was to protect Blake from physical harm and legal entanglements. When family members take matters into their own hands, it is likely that they will make matters worse. They may even become targets of the legal system. This is a sure way to complicate the recovery of a rape victim.

Paul and Blake's reactions to the rape had an equally troubling impact on the younger children. Constant racial slurs and an interpretation of the rape strictly on the basis of race made the children unduly fearful and angry toward all blacks.

A generalized anxiety toward an entire group of people, based upon the assumption that they are all basically alike, is highly debilitating; an impediment to daily functioning. In the case of Karen, her previously friendly relationships with blacks suffered. In addition, her fear toward black males was developing into an unhealthy preoccupation. Such feelings probably would not have emerged if Paul and Blake had responded differently.

Also tragic is what happened to Tim. His actions grew out of the strong pressure for revenge against blacks that he felt at home. Certainly his beliefs about black people were based on inaccurate assumptions and tended to reflect the perpetual tensions of his home life. His actions in vandalizing the lockers at school only functioned to identify him as a trouble maker in the eyes of authorities. This had serious negative consequences for his subsequent academic performance. Unfortunately, Tim's father and older brother reinforced the very behavior which hurt both him and his mother.

In the final analysis, Barbara's recovery was complicated and prolonged by the behavior of Paul and Blake. She was made to assume the added burden of worrying about their safety, as well as the disturbing behaviors of the children. The atmosphere in the home caused by her husband and her elder son made it difficult for the family to function effectively. They were all hurt.

What Paul and Blake Should Have Done

- **Paul and Blake should have focused their attention upon Barbara's needs. They should have left the issue of justice to the authorities**. Because Paul and Blake were so caught up in

seeking revenge they neglected to provide the love
and support which a rape victim desperately needs.

• **Paul and Blake should have realized that all men
of any race are not rapists.** They should have communicated this to Barbara and the children. Such
a generalization was very unfair and intensified
existing racial prejudices. It also increased the
family's anxiety and disrupted their lives.

• **Paul and Blake should have channeled their
energy toward assisting in Barbara's recovery.**
They could have suggested professional counseling
for Barbara. They could also have considered
counseling for themselves to help them resolve their
anger and frustration. This would have removed
a large burden from Barbara, who became very
concerned for her family's safety.

Case Study 5

Lori: Rape Victim With
Supportive Partner

The Incident

Lori is an attractive 24 year old woman who is employed
as a distributor for a large textbook company. On an evening
in March, Lori was returning to her apartment after a lengthy
sales meeting. When she parked her car and opened the door
a man appeared out of nowhere and grabbed her by the arm.
He displayed a knife and forced her to drive with him to a
deserted spot. He explained to her that they were going to
"have some fun." If she screamed or in any way resisted,
he would use the knife on her.

Although she did not suffer severe physical injury, Lori was subjected to extreme terror, vulgar language and degrading sexual acts. At no time during the rape did Lori feel she could effectively use force to resist the assault. However, she did plead with him (without success) to let her go. Even though the event seemed to her like a fragmented nightmare, Lori had the presence of mind to take mental notes that later proved helpful to the police. After the attack, despite the fact that she felt "filthy," she went directly to the police without bathing or changing clothing. Lori was aware of the importance of physical evidence and was determined to see the rapist punished.

Others React

After a brief preliminary report, Lori was taken directly to a hospital for examination and treatment. Up until this point, Lori had remained remarkably controlled. However, it was at the hospital that she began to show signs of the emotional strain. This stress was further compounded by the actions of those who were supposed to help her. Lori was made to wait in the emergency room in her disheveled condition for nearly one hour. She was then examined by a male doctor. He was professional in demeanor, but did not appear to be sensitive to her emotional state. The series of rape examination procedures, though routine to the doctor, were discomforting to Lori and added to her distress. During this time, she was deeply concerned about the potential responses of her family and of John, her fiance, who as yet had not been informed of what happened.

When the medical examination had been completed, Lori was taken home by a police officer and allowed to bathe and change clothing. It was requested that she return to the police station that evening to provide a full account of the event. While at home Lori telephoned her fiance to briefly explain what happened. She asked him to meet her at the police station. Although John was very upset and wanted her to explain more fully what had happened, he agreed to meet her as requested.

When John arrived at the police station, Lori was being questioned by detectives. As he sat waiting for her, John felt angry, hurt, confused and highly apprehensive. He did not know what to expect. He was concerned about how this incident would change his relationship with Lori. As Lori emerged from the room where she was questioned, John held out his arms and they embraced without saying a word. Lori began to cry. Although John also felt like crying, he held her and told her how much he loved her. John wanted very much for Lori to tell him what happened, but he sensed that this was not the appropriate time for such a discussion.

When the police finished questioning her, John took Lori back to her apartment and offered to make her a hot meal. Although Lori seemed silent and distant, he realized that her silence was not an attempt to shut him out, but rather an understandable response to what had happened. It was then that John held her hand and said: "Look, I'm just as confused about this as you. I want to know what happened to you. However, I realize you may need some time to sort things out. Whenever you're ready, I'm willing to listen. I also want you to know that I don't blame you for what happened. You shouldn't blame yourself either. All that really matters is that you are OK; that we love each other. This is going to be hard on both of us but if we trust and help each other, I know we can get through it."

Lori was visibly relieved by what John said. However, she was very anxious about how her parents would react to news of the rape. John asked her if she would like him to break the news to her family. Together they discussed various approaches. Lori decided that John would tell her family and, when she was ready, they would both answer any questions her parents had.

In part as a result of his support and the support of her family, Lori decided to press charges against the rapist. The case was scheduled for trial and John was understanding and supportive of Lori's decision to pursue legal action. John took time off from work to be with her during the trial. They were married that fall.

Lessons To Be Learned

John's behavior throughout Lori's ordeal suggests a high level of emotional security and self-awareness. John had no difficulty in understanding that she was a victim and therefore not responsible for what happened. He did not question her judgment nor her inability to physically resist the assault. Although he did have questions about what happened to her, he did not pressure her into talking about the incident. He didn't pressure her after she was ready either. John showed great patience and sensitivity by giving Lori's immediate needs a higher priority than his own.

Of equal importance to Lori's recovery was the fact that John communicated in clear terms to her that he did not hold her responsible for what occurred. He let her know that his love for her was unchanged. John also let her know that he was willing to help her and stick by her throughout the legal process. John's assistance in approaching Lori's family demonstrated his support. In a way, Lori's victimization dramatically proved John's love and trust. Their relationship was actually strengthened by the experience. Lori, as a result, was able to reclaim her health much sooner than is typical for many women following the horrid crime of rape.

What John Did

John clearly was an important asset in Lori's recovery. Husbands, fathers and male friends have much to offer recovering rape victims if they follow John's example.

- **John placed Lori's needs ahead of his own.** Because Lori was not distracted by John's struggles, she focused her full attention on her own feelings and recovery.

- **John provided support but followed Lori's cues.** While he offered advice he allowed Lori to make her own decisions.

- **At no time did John suggest or imply that Lori was responsible for her victimization.**

- **John was helpful in communicating with Lori's family.** By doing so, he served as a buffer and further demonstrated his support for Lori.

- **John demonstrated his support for Lori by taking time off from work to be with her during the trial.**

- **Throughout the entire ordeal John's presence and support assured Lori that she was not alone.** This was his greatest contribution.

Appendix B
Rape Crisis Centers

ALABAMA

Birmingham

Rape Response Program
3600 8th Ave S.
Birmingham, AL 35222
(205) 323-7273
24-hour hotline

Montgomery

Council Against
Rape/Lighthouse
830 S Court St.,
P.O. Box 4622
Montgomery, AL 36104
(205) 263-4481
9:00 am-7:00 pm
24-hour services (through
referral network)

Tuscaloosa

Indian Rivers Community
Mental Health Center
1915 6th St.
Tuscaloosa, AL 35403
(205) 345-1600
8:00 am-5:00 pm Mon, Tues,
Thurs, Fri;
8:00 am-6:00 pm Wed
24-Hour Hotline

ALASKA

Anchorage

Standing Together Against
Rape
430 W. 7th Ave., Suite 205
Anchorage, AK 99510
(907) 276-7273 (hotline)
(907) 277-0222 (week nights,
weekends)
24-hour hotline

Fairbanks

Women in Crisis—Counseling and
Assistance, Inc.
(WICCA)
331 Fifth Ave.
Fairbanks, AK 99701
(907) 452-7273 (hotline)
(907) 452-2293 (office)
24-hour hotline

Nome

Bering Sea Women's Group
P.O. Box 1596
Nome, AK 99762
(907) 443-5444
24-hour hotline

ARIZONA

Flagstaff

Coconino Community
Guidance Center, Inc.
519 N. Leroux
Flagstaff, AZ 86001
(602) 774-3351
24-hour hotline

Phoenix

Center Against Sexual Assault
(CASA)
1131 E. Missouri
Phoenix, AZ 85014
(602) 257-8095 (hotline)
(602) 279-9824 (office)
8:30 am-7:00 pm
24-hour hotline

Tucson

Tucson Rape Crisis
Center, Inc.
P.O. Box 843
Tucson, AZ 87502
(602) 623-7273 (hotline)
(602) 624-7273 (office)
24-hour hotline

ARKANSAS

Little Rock

Rape Crisis, Inc.
P.O. Box 5181,
Hillcrest Station
Little Rock, AR 72205
(501) 375-5181
24-hour hotline

CALIFORNIA

Anaheim

Rape Crisis Network Unit
503 N. Anaheim Blvd.
Anaheim, CA 92805
(714) 776-3004
9:00 am-5:00 pm

Berkeley

Bay Area Women Against Rape
P.O. Box 240
Berkeley, CA 94703
(415) 845-7273
24-hour hotline

National Clearinghouse
on Marital Rape (NCOMR)
2325 Oak St.
Berkeley, CA 94708
(415) 548-1770

Fresno

Rape Counseling Service
of Fresno, Inc.
1660 M. St.
Fresno, CA 93721
(209) 222-7273 (hotline)
(209) 486-4692 (office)
8:30 am-5:00 pm
24-hour hotline

Irvine

Irvine Community Against
Rape Everywhere
(I.C.A.R.E.)
P.O. Box 4031
Irvine, CA 92717
(714) 830-6111
24-hour hotline

Laguna Beach

Laguna Beach Free Clinic
Rape Crisis Unit
460 Ocean Ave.
Laguna Beach, CA 92651
(714) 494-0761
24-hour hotline

Monterey

Rape Crisis Center of
the Monterey Peninsula
P.O. Box 862
Monterey, CA 93940
(408) 375-4357
24-hour hotline

Long Beach

Long Beach Rape Hotline
P.O. Box 14377
Long Beach, CA 90803
(213) 597-2002
24-hour hotline

Orange

Orange County Rape
Crisis Hotline
P.O. Box 2572
Orange, CA 92669
(714) 831-9110
24-hour hotline

Los Angeles

East Los Angeles Rape Crisis
Center, Inc.
P.O. Box 63245
Los Angeles, CA 90063
(213) 262-0944
(bilingual hotline)
(213) 267-2824 (office)
24-hour hotline

Palo Alto

Mid-Peninsula Rape
Crisis Center
4161 Alma St.
Palo Alto, CA 94306
(415) 493-7273 (hotline)
(415) 494-0972 (office)
24-hour hotline

Rape Response Service
Thalians Community Mental
Health Center
Cedar-Sinai Medical Center
8730 Alden Dr.
Los Angeles, CA 90048
(213) 855-3506 (hotline)
(213) 855-3530 (office)
24-hour hotline

Pasadena

Rape Emergency Assistance
Crisis Telephone (REACT)
Pasadena-Foothill Valley
YWCA
78 N. Marengo Ave.
Pasadena, CA 91101
(213) 973-3385 (hotline)
(213) 973-5171 (office)
24-hour hotline

Riverside

Riverside Area
Rape Crisis Center
3775 14th St.
Riverside, CA 92501
(714) 686-7273
24-hour hotline

Sacramento

Sacramento Rape
Crisis Center
2104 Capitol Ave.
Sacramento, CA 95816
(916) 447-7273 (hotline)
(916) 447-3223 (office)
24-hour hotline

San Bernardino

San Bernardino Rape Crisis
Intervention Services
1875 N "D" St.
San Bernardino, CA 92405
(714) 882-5291 (hotline)
(714) 883-8689 (office)
9:00 am-5:00 pm
24-hour hotline

San Francisco

San Francisco Women
Against Rape
3543 18th St.
San Francisco, CA 94110
(415) 647-7273
3:00 pm-7:00 am (counseling)
24-hour hotline

Sexual Trauma Services
50 Ivy St.
San Francisco, CA 94121
(415) 558-3824
24-hour hotline

University of California
Rape Treatment Center
401 Parnassus Ave.
San Francisco, CA 94143
(414) 681-8080, ext. 394
24-hour hotline

San Jose

Rape Prevention
and Education Committee
San Jose State University
Counseling Services, Adm 201
San Jose, CA 95192
(408) 277-2262
9:00 am-5:00 pm
24-hour hotline

YWCA—Valley Rape
Crisis Center
375 S. 3rd St.
San Jose, CA 95112
(408) 287-3000 (hotline)
(408) 295-4011 (office)
8:30 am-5:00 pm
24-hour hotline

San Mateo

San Mateo Women
Against Rape
P.O. Box 6299
San Mateo, CA 94401
(415) 349-7273
24-hour hotline

San Rafael

Marin Rape Crisis Center
P.O. Box 392
San Rafael, CA 94902
(415) 924-2100
24-hour hotline

Santa Cruz

Santa Cruz Women
Against Rape
P.O. Box 711
Santa Cruz, CA 95061
(408) 426-7273
24-hour hotline

Santa Monica

Rape Treatment Center
Santa Monica Hospital
Medical Center
1225 15th St.
Santa Monica, CA 90404
(213) 451-1511
24-hour services

Santa Rosa

Rape Crisis Center
of Sonoma County
P.O. Box 1426
Santa Rosa, CA 95402
(707) 545-7273 (hotline)
(707) 545-7270 (office)
9:00 am-5:00 pm
24-hour hotline

Stockton

Rape Crisis Center
of San Joaquin County
P.O. Box 4803
Stockton, CA 95204
(209) 465-4997 (hotline)
(209) 465-8969 (office)
24-hour hotline

COLORADO

Colorado Springs

Rape Crisis Service
12 N. Meade St.
Colorado Springs, CO 80909
(303) 471-4357 (hotline)
(303) 633-4601 (office)
24-hour hotline

Denver

Rape Crisis Program
Denver General Hospital
7th and Cherokee
Denver, CO 80204
(303) 893-6000
24-hour services

Grand Junction

Rape Crisis Center
1059 Rood
Grand Junction, CO 81501
(303) 243-0190
24-hour hotline

CONNECTICUT

Bridgeport

Rape Crisis Service
YWCA of Greater Bridgeport
1862 E. Main St.
Bridgeport, CT 06610
(203) 333-2233 (hotline)
(203) 334-6154 (Office)
24-hour hotline

Hartford

Sexual Assault Crisis
Service/YWCA
135 Broad St.
Hartford, CT 06105
(203) 522-6666 (hotline)
(203) 525-1163,
ext. 205 (office)
24-hour hotline

New Haven

Rape Crisis Center
148 Orange St.
New Haven, CT 06510
(203) 397-2273
24-hour hotline

Stamford

Rape Crisis Service
of Stamford
322 Main St.
Stamford, CT 06820
(203) 329-2929 (hotline)
(203) 348-9346 (office)
9:00 am-5:00 pm
24-hour hotline

DELAWARE

Newark

Support Group for Victims
of Sexual Offense (S.O.S.)
Laurel Hall
University of Delaware
Newark, DE 19711
(302) 738-2226 (hotline)
(302) 738-1202 (office)
24-hour hotline

Wilmington

Rape Crisis Center
of Wilmington
P.O. Box 1507
Wilmington, DE 19899
(302) 658-5011
24-hour hotline

DISTRICT OF COLUMBIA
(WASHINGTON, DC)

Feminist Alliance Against
Rape (FAAR)
P.O. Box 21033
Washington, DC 20009
(202) 462-3717

Sexual Assault Program
Women's Medical Center
of Washington, DC
1712 I Street NW, Suite 704
Washington, DC 20006
(202) 298-9227
(202) 298-6655 (teletype
for hearing-impaired)
9:00 am-5:00 pm Mon-Sat

FLORIDA

Fort Lauderdale

Victim Advocate Office
Fort Lauderdale
Police Department
1300 W. Broward Blvd.
Fort Lauderdale, FL 33312
(305) 761-2143
24-hour services

Jacksonville

Rape Crisis Center
Emergency Treatment Unit
Community Mental
Health Center
University Hospital
655 W. 8th St.
Jacksonville, FL 32209
(904) 358-3272, ext. 2533
24-hour hotline

Melrose

Sexual Assault Research
Association (Rape) (SARA)
P.O. Box 738
Melrose, FL 32666
(904) 475-1859

Miami

Rape Treatment Center
1611 NW 12th Ave.
Miami, FL 33136
(305) 325-6949
24-hour hotline

Orlando

Rape Crisis
Intervention Program
Orlando Regional
Medical Center
1414 S. Kuhl Ave.
Orlando, FL 32802
(305) 841-5111
24-hour services

Pensacola

Rape Crisis Center
of West Florida
YWCA 1417 N. 12th Ave.
Pensacola, FL 32503
(904) 433-7273
24-hour hotline

Tampa

Women's Center of Tampa,
Inc.
609 DeLeon St.
Tampa, FL 33606
(813) 251-8629

West Palm Beach

Sexual Assault
Assistance Project
Pan-Am Bldg., Rm. 308
307 N. Dixie Hwy.
West Palm Beach, FL 33401
(305) 833-7273 (hotline)
(305) 837-2073 (office)
24-hour hotline

104

GEORGIA

Atlanta

Rape Crisis Center
Grady Memorial Hospital
80 Butler St., SE
Atlanta, GA 30303
(404) 588-4861
24-hour hotline

Augusta

Augusta Rape Crisis Line
P.O. Box 3474
Hill Station
Augusta, GA 30904
(404) 724-5200
24-hour hotline

Savannah

Rape Crisis Center of
the Coastal Empire, Inc.
P.O. Box 8492
Savannah, GA 31412
(912) 233-7273
24-hour hotline

HAWAII

Honolulu

Alternatives for
Women Program
Diamond Head Mental
Health Center
550 Makapuu Ave.
Honolulu, HI 96816
(808) 737-5465
8:00 am-4:30 pm

IDAHO

Boise

Rape Crisis Alliance
720 Washington St.
Boise, ID 83702
(208) 345-7273
24-hour hotline

Moscow

Women's Center
University of Idaho
Moscow, ID 83843
(208) 885-6616
8:00 am-5:00 pm

Pocatello

Rape Crisis Team
Women's Advocates
454 N. Garfield
Pocatello, ID 83201
(208) 232-9169
24-hour hotline

ILLINOIS

Chicago

Chicago Women Aginst Rape
Loop YWCA—Women's
Services
37 S. Wabash
Chicago, IL 60603
(312) 372-6600, ext. 61
9:00 am-5:00 pm

Illinois Crime Victims
Compensation Program
188 W. Randolph St.,
Suite 2200
Chicago, IL 60601
(312) 793-2585
8:30 am-5:15 pm

Rape Victim Advocates
P.O. Box 11537
Chicago, IL 60611
(312) 883-5688
on call 24 hours

Decatur

Citizens Against Rape
436 N. Main St.
Decatur, IL 62521
(217) 429-7444
24-hour hotline

Edwardsville

Rape and Sexual Abuse
Care Center
Southern Illinois University
at Edwardsville
166 Bluff Rd., P.O. Box 154
Edwardsville, IL 62026
(618) 692-2197
9:00 am-5:00 pm
24-hour hotline

Joliet

Will County Rape
Crisis Center
P.O. Box 354
Joliet, IL 60435
(815) 722-3344 (hotline)
(815) 744-5280 (office)
24-hour hotline

Rockford

Rockford Rape Counseling
Center, Inc.
P.O. Box 4027
Rockford, IL 61110
(815) 964-4044 (hotline)
(815) 962-3268 (office)
24-hour hotline

Springfield

Rape Information and
Counseling Service
(RICS)
P.O. Box 2211
Springfield, IL 62705
(217) 753-8081 (hotline)
(217) 753-0133 (office)
24-hour hotline

INDIANA

Elkhart

SUPPORT YWCA Women's
Resource Center
122 W. Lexington Ave.
Elkhart, IN 46514
(219) 293-8671
24-hour hotline

Fort Wayne

Rape Crisis Center, Inc.
P.O. Box 5367
Fort Wayne, IN 46805
(219) 426-7273
24-hour hotline

Gary

Calumet Women United
Against Rape
P.O. Box 2617
Gary, IN 46403
(219) 937-0450, 980-4207 and
769-3141 (local hotlines)
24-hour hotlines

Indianapolis

Crisis and Suicide
Intervention Service
Mental Health Association
1433 N. Meridian St.
Rm. 202
Indianapolis, IN 46202
(317) 632-7575
24-hour hotline

Terre Haute

Lifeline
679 Ohio St.
Terre Haute, IN 47807
(812) 235-8333 (hotline)
(812) 238-2620 (office)
24-hour hotline

South Bend

Women's Committee
on Sex Offense
Sex Offense Staff (S.O.S.)
P.O. Box 931
South Bend, IN 46624
(219) 232-3344 (hotline)
(219) 234-0061,
ext. 210 (office)
24-hour hotline

IOWA

Ames

Story County Sexual Assault
Care Center
P.O. Box 1150, ISU Station
Ames, IA 50010
(515) 292-1101
24-hour hotline

Cedar Rapids

Rape Crisis Services—YWCA
318 5th St., SE
Cedar Rapids, IA 52401
(319) 398-3955 (hotline)
(319) 365-1458 (YWCA)
24-hour hotline

Iowa City

Rape Victim Advocacy Program
130 N Madison St.
Iowa City, IA 52240
(319) 338-4800
24-hour hotline

KANSAS

Kansas City

Police Public Education
No. 1 Civic Center Plaza
Kansas City, KS 66101
(913) 371-2000, ext. 507
8:00 am-4:00 pm

Lawrence

Douglas County Rape Victim
Support Service, Inc.
1035 Pennsylvania
Lawrence, KS 66044
(913) 841-2345 (hotline)
(913) 843-8985 (office)
1:00 pm-4:00 pm
24-hour hotline

Manhattan

Regional Crisis Center for
Victims of Family Abuse
or Rape
P.O. Box 164
Manhattan, KS 66502
(913) 539-2785
24-hour hotline

Topeka

Can Help
P.O. Box 1364
Topeka, KS 66601
(913) 295-8499
24-hour hotline

Wichita

Wichita Area
Rape Center, Inc.
1801 E 10th St.
Wichita, KS 67214
(316) 263-3002 (hotline)
(316) 263-0185 (office)
8:30 am-5:00 pm
24-hour hotline

KENTUCKY

Ashland

Lansdowne Mental Health
Center—Emergency Service
2162 Greenup Ave.
Ashland, KY 41101
(606) 324-1141
24-hour hotline

Lexington

Lexington Rape Crisis Center
P.O. Box 1603
Lexington, KY 40592
(606) 253-2511
8:00 am-5:00 pm
24-hour hotline

Louisville

R.A.P.E. Relief Center
604 S. 3rd St.
Louisville, KY 40202
(502) 581-7273
24-hour hotline

LOUISIANA

Baton Rouge

Stop Rape Crisis Center
East Baton Rouge Parish
District Attorney's Office
215 St. Louis St., #307
Baton Rouge, LA 70801
(504) 389-3456
24-hour hotline

New Orleans

YWCA Rape Crisis Service
601 S. Jefferson David Pkwy.
New Orleans, LA 70119
(504) 821-6000 (hotline)
(504) 488-2693 (office)
9:00 am-5:00 pm
24-hour hotline

Shreveport

Women's Resource Center
of the YWCA
710 Travis St.
Shreveport, LA 71101
(318) 222-0556 (hotline)
(318) 222-2116 (office)
24-hour hotline

MAINE

Portland

The Rape Crisis Center
of Greater Portland
193 Middle St.
Portland, ME 04101
(207) 774-3613 (hotline)
(207) 774-4305 (office)
24-hour hotline

MARYLAND

Baltimore

Baltimore Center for Victims
of Sexual Assault
128 W. Franklin St.
Baltimore, MD 21201
(301) 366-7273
24-hour hotline

Bethesda

Community Crisis Center
Sexual Assault Services
4910 Auburn Ave.
Bethesda, MD 20014
(301) 656-9449 (hotline)
(301) 656-9526 (office)
24-hour hotline

College Park

Women's Crisis Hotline
University of Maryland
Health Center, Rm. 3114
College Park, MD 20742
(301) 454-4616 or 454-4617
10:00 am-6:00 pm

Columbia

Howard County Rape
Crisis Center
P.O. Box 201
Columbia, MD 21045
(301) 997-3292 (hotline)
(301) 997-2502 (office)
24-hour hotline

MASSACHUSETTS

Amherst

Counselors/Advocates
Against Rape
40 Everywoman's Center,
Wilder Hall
University of Massachusetts
Amherst, MA 01003
(413) 545-0800 (hotline)
(413) 545-0883 (office)
24-hour hotline

Boston

Rape Crisis
Intervention Program
Beth Israel Hospital
330 Brookline Ave.
Boston, MA 02215
(617) 735-3337 (emergency)
(617) 735-4645 (information)
9:00 am-5:00 pm
24-hour services

Cambridge

Boston Area Rape
Crisis Center
Women's Center
46 Pleasant St.
Cambridge, MA 02139
(617) 492-7273
24-hour hotline

Springfield

Hotline to End Rape
and Abuse (HERA)
26 Howard St.
Springfield, MA 01105
(413) 733-2561
24-hour hotline

Worcester

Rape Crisis Program
162 Chandler St.
Worcester, MA 01609
(617) 799-5700 (hotline)
(617) 756-4354 (office)
24-hour hotline

MICHIGAN

Ann Arbor

Women's Crisis Center
211½ N. 4th Ave.
Ann Arbor, MI 48107
(313) 995-9100 (hotline)
(313) 761-9475 (office)
10:00 am-10:00 pm

Detroit

Rape Counseling Center
Detroit Police Department
1326 St. Antoine, Rm. 828
Detroit, MI 48207
(313) 224-4487 (day hotline)
(313) 224-0550 (night hotline)
(313) 963-4649 (office)
24-hour hotline

East Lansing

Sexual Assault Counseling
of The Listening Ear
547½ E. Grand River Ave.
East Lansing, MI 48823
(517) 337-1717
24-hour hotline

Flint

Sexual Assault Crisis Center
YWCA
310 E. 3rd St.
Flint, MI 48502
(313) 767-2662
9:00 am-5:00 pm
24-hour hotline

Grand Rapids

Rape Crisis Team
750 Cherry, SE
Grand Rapids, MI 49503
(616) 774-3535
24-hour hotline

Kalamazoo

Kalamazoo Sexual Assault
Program
211 S. Rose St.
Kalamazoo, MI 49006
(616) 565-7199
24-hour hotline

Muskegon

Rape/Spouse Assault Crisis
Center of EveryWoman's
Place, Inc.
29 Strong Ave.
Muskegon, MI 49441
(616) 722-3333 (hotline)
(616) 726-4493 (office)
9:00 am-5:00 pm
24-hour hotline

Saginaw

Saginaw County Rape
Crisis Center, Inc.
1765 E. Genesee St.
Saginaw, MI 48601
(517) 755-6565
9:00 am-11:00 pm Mon-Fri;
12:00 noon-1:00 am Sat-Sun
24-hour hotline

MINNESOTA

Alexandria

Listening Ear Crisis Center
111 17th Ave. E.
Alexandria, MN 56308
(612) 763-6638
24-hour hotline

Bemidji

Beltrami County Sexual
Assault Task Force
Box 1112
Bemidji, MN 56601
(218) 586-2448
24-hour hotline

Duluth

Aid to Victims
of Sexual Assault
2 E. 5th St.
Duluth, MN 55805
(218) 727-8538
(hotline-Duluth)
(800) 232-1300 (toll-free)
(218) 727-4353 (office)
8:00 am-4:30 pm
24-hour hotline

Minneapolis

Rape and Sexual
Assault Center
1222 W. 31st St.
Minneapolis, MN 55408
(612) 825-4357
9:00 am-7:30 pm
24-hour hotline

St. Cloud

Rape Crisis Service
1900 Minnesota Blvd.
St. Cloud, MN 56301
(612) 251-4357
24-hour hotline

St. Paul

Minnesota Program for
Victims of Sexual Assault
Minnesota State Department
of Corrections
430 Metro Square Bldg.
St. Paul, MN 55101
(612) 296-7084
8:00 am-5:00 pm

National Coalition Against
Sexual Assault
(Rape)(NCASA)
c/o Minnesota Program for
Victims of Sexual Assault
430 Metro Square Bldg.
St. Paul, MN 55101
(612) 296-7084

Winona

Sexual Assault Crisis Aid
205 Exchange Bldg.
Winona, MN 55987
(507) 452-4440
24-hour hotline

MISSISSIPPI

Hattiesburg

National Organization
of Victim Assistance
P.O. Box 9227,
Southern Station
Hattiesburg, MS 39401
(601) 266-4100
8:00 am-5:00 pm

Jackson

Rape Crisis Center
P.O. Box 4174
Jackson, MS 39216
(601) 354-1113 (hotline)
(601) 354-5304 (office)
24-hour hotline

MISSOURI

Columbia

Abuse, Assault, and Rape
Crisis Center (AARCC)
P.O. Box 1827
Columbia, MO 65201
(314) 442-3322 (hotline)
(314) 449-7721 (office)
12:00 noon-4:00 pm
24-hour hotline

Kansas City

Sexual Assault
Treatment Center
St. Lukes Hospital
Emergency Room
4400 Wornall Rd.
Kansas City, MO 64111
(816) 932-2171
24-hour services

St. Louis

Aid to Victims of Crime
607 N. Grand Blvd.
St. Louis, MO 63103
(314) 531-2597
8:00 am-5:00 pm

Springfield

Rape Crisis Assistance, Inc.
430 S. Ave., 7th Floor
Springfield, MO 65806
(417) 866-1969, ext. 66
24-hour hotline

MONTANA

Billings

Billings Rape Task Force
1245 N. 29th St., Rm. 218
Billings, MT 59101
(406) 259-6506
24-hour hotline

Helena

Violence Against Women
Crisis Line and Program
Rape Awareness Program
Helena Woman's Center
146 E. 6th Ave.
Helena, MT 59601
(406) 443-5353
24-hour hotline

NEBRASKA

Lincoln

Rape/Spouse Abuse
Crisis Center
33 H St.
Lincoln, NE 68508
(402) 475-7273
24-hour hotline

Omaha

Women Against Violence
YWCA
3929 Harney St. Rm. 100
Omaha, NE 68131
(402) 345-7273 (hotline)
(402) 342-2748 (office)
9:00 am-5:00 pm
24-hour hotline

NEVADA

Las Vegas

Community Action
Against Rape
749 Veterans Memorial Dr.,
Rm. 150
Las Vegas, NV 89101
(702) 735-1111 (hotline)
(702) 385-0471 (office)
24-hour hotline

NEW HAMPSHIRE

Concord

INFO-LINE
New Hampshire Social
Welfare Council, Inc.
20 S. Main St., Box 1255
Concord, NH 03301
(800) 852-3311
(New Hampshire only)
(603) 228-0571
24-hour hotline

Portsmouth

Rape and Assault Prevention
Program
Portsmouth Police Department
28 Penhallow St.
Portsmouth, NH 03801
(603) 436-2145
24-hour services

NEW JERSEY

Hackensack

Supporting the Elimination
of Rape, Violence and
Exploitation (S.E.R.V.E.)
191 Main St.
Hackensack, NJ 07601
(201) 343-3043
9:00 am-5:00 pm
24-hour hotline

New Brunswick

Women's Crisis Center
56 College Ave.
New Brunswick, NJ 08904
(201) 828-7273
24-hour hotline

Newark

Sexual Assault Rape Analysis
Unit (S.A.R.A.)
22 Franklin St.
Newark, NJ 07102
(201) 733-7273
9:00 am-2:00 am
24-hour hotline

Trenton

NOW—New Jersey Rape
Task Force
NOW Office
32 W. Lafayette St.
Trenton, NJ 08618
(609) 393-7474

NEW MEXICO

Albuquerque

Albuquerque Rape Crisis
Center
917 Vassar, NE
Albuquerque, NM 87106
(505) 247-0707 (hotline)
(505) 242-4619 (office)
8:00 am-5:00 pm
24-hour hotline

Women's Center
University of New Mexico
1824 Las Lomas, NE
Albuquerque, NM 87106
(505) 277-3716
8:00 am-5:00 pm

114   *IF SHE IS RAPED*

Carlsbad

Carlsbad Area Rape
Crisis Center
Carlsbad Area Counseling
and Resource Center
701 N. Canal
Carlsbad, NM 88220
(505) 885-8888 (hotline)
(505) 887-0493 (office)
24-hour hotline

Espanola

Rape Counseling Program
Counseling Services of
Northern New Mexico
816 Los Alamos Hwy.
Espanola, NM 87532
(505) 753-6985 (hotline)
(505) 753-6583 (office)
9:00 am-5:00 pm Mon-Fri
24-hour hotline

Santa Fe

Santa Fe Rape Crisis
Center, Inc.
839 Harvey Building, Suite B
Paseo de Peralta
Santa Fe, NM 87501
(505) 982-4667
8:30 am-5:00 pm
24-hour hotline

Taos

Community Against
Rape, Inc.
Box 3170
Taos, NM 87571
(505) 758-2910
24-hour hotline

NEW YORK

Binghamton

Rape Crisis Center
56-58 Whitney Ave.
Binghamton, NY 13904
(607) 722-4256
8:30 am-6:00 pm
24-hour hotline

Bronx

Borough Crisis Center
Mayor's Task Force on Rape
Lincoln Hospital
234 E. 149th St.
Bronx, NY 10451
(212) 579-5326, 579-5327
or 579-5328
24-hour hotline

Brooklyn

Borough Crisis Center
Mayor's Task Force on Rape
Kings County Hospital
451 Clarkson Ave. (C Bldg.)
Brooklyn, NY 11203
(212) 735-2424, 735-2425
or 735-2426
24-hour hotline

Buffalo

Rape Prevention: Campus
and Community
Department of Public Safety
Buffalo State College
1300 Elmwood Ave.
110 Chase Hall
Buffalo, NY 14222
(716) 878-6333

New York

Borough Crisis Center
Mayor's Task Force on Rape
Harlem Hospital
506 Lenox Ave.
New York, NY 10037
(212) 694-8251, 694-8252
or 694-8253
24-hour hotline

Mayor's Task Force on Rape,
Central Office
2 Lafayette St., 3rd Floor
New York, NY 10805
(212) 566-1010
9:00 am-5:00 p.m.

National Board YWCA of the
U.S.A.
600 Lexington Ave.
New York, NY 10022
(212) 753-4700
8:45 am-4:45 pm

Victim Services Agency,
Inc.—Hotline
2 Lafayette St.
New York, NY 10007
(212) 577-7777 (hotline)
(212) 577-7700 (office)
9:00 am-12:00 midnight
24-hour hotline

Niagara Falls

Niagara County Task Force
on Rape
Niagara Falls Memorial
Medical Center
621 Tenth St.
Niagara Falls, NY 14302
(716) 278-4528
8:30 am-4:30 pm

Rochester

Rape Crisis Service of Planned
Parenthood of
Rochester and Monroe County
24 Windsor St.
Rochester, NY 14605
(716) 546-2595
24-hour hotline

Schenectady

Rape Crisis Service of
Schenectady, Inc.
YWCA
44 Washington Ave.
Schenectady, NY 12305
(518) 346-2266
24-hour hotline

Syracuse

Rape Crisis Center of
Syracuse, Inc.
304 Seymour St.
Syracuse, NY 13204
(315) 422-7273
8:30 am-5:00 pm
24-hour hotline

NORTH CAROLINA

Asheville

Rape Crisis Center of
Asheville
331 College St.
Allen Center
Asheville, NC 28801
(704) 255-7576
24-hour hotline

Burlington

Rape Crisis Alliance of
Alamance County
Box 652
Burlington, NC 27215
(919) 227-6220
24-hour hotline

Chapel Hill

Chapel Hill—Carrboro Rape
Crisis Center
Box 871
Chapel Hill, NC 27514
(919) 967-7273 (hotline)
(919) 929-0471, ext. 240
(office)
10:00 am-2:00 pm
24-hour hotline

Charlotte

Charlotte-Mecklenburg Rape
Crisis Service
P.O. Box 29055
Charlotte, NC 28212
(704) 373-0982
24-hour hotline

Durham

Durham Rape Crisis Center
P.O. Box 2491, West Durham
Station
Durham, NC 27705
(919) 688-4353
24-hour hotline

Greensboro

Rape: Action, Prevention,
Education Center, Inc. of
Greensboro, NC
314 N. Davie St.
Greensboro, NC 27401
(919) 273-7273 (hotline)
(919) 379-5229 (office)
24-hour hotline

Raleigh

Rape Crisis Center of Raleigh
P.O. Box 5223
Raleigh, NC 27650
(919) 782-3060
24-hour hotline

Winston-Salem

Winston Women Against
Rape/Rape Line
P.O. Box 5980
Winston-Salem, NC 27103
(919) 723-5494
(919) 724-7911 (Tele—Med
Tape: Rape, A Crime of
Violence Against Women;
ask for tape number 899)
8:00 am-5:00 pm
24-hour hotline

NORTH DAKOTA

Fargo

Rape and Abuse Crisis Center
of Fargo-Moorhead
P.O. Box 1655
Fargo, ND 58102
(701) 293-7273
24-hour hotline

Grand Forks

Grand Forks Rape Crisis
Center
118 N. 3rd St., Box 1695
Grand Forks, ND 58201
(701) 746-6666 (hotline)
(701) 772-8171 (office)
24-hour hotline

OHIO

Akron

Akron Rape Crisis Center
St. Paul's Episcopal Church
1361 W. Market St.
Akron, OH 44313
(216) 434-7273
24-hour hotline

Cincinnati

Women Helping Women, Inc.
9th and Walnut Sts.
Cincinnati, OH 45202
(513) 381-5610 (hotline)
(513) 381-6003 (office)
24-hour hotline

Cleveland

Community Guidance and
Human Services Mental
Health Center
3740 Euclid
Cleveland, OH 44115
(216) 431-7774
8:30 am-5:00 pm
Mon-Wed, Fri;
8:30 am-9:00 pm Thurs
24-hour services

Columbus

Women Against Rape
P.O. Box 02084
Columbus, OH 43202
(614) 221-4447 (hotline)
(614) 291-9751 (information)
24-hour hotline

Dayton

EASTWAY Community
Mental Health Center
1040 S. Smithville Rd.
Dayton, OH 45403
(513) 254-8406
24-hour services

Springfield

Project Woman Rape and
Battered Victims Crisis Center
1101 E. High St.
Springfield, OH 45501
(513) 325-3707
24-hour hotline

Toledo

Toledo United Against Rape
P.O. Box 4372,
1723 Broadway
Toledo, OH 43609
(419) 475-0494
24-hour hotline

118

IF SHE IS RAPED

OKLAHOMA

Norman

Women's Resource Center
207½ E. Gray, P.O. Box 474
Norman, OK 73071
(405) 364-9424
8:00 am-5:00 pm Mon-Fri
24-hour hotline

Oklahoma City

Rape Victim Assistance
57th and N. Shartel
Oklahoma City, OK 73118
Mailing Address: P.O. Box 765
Bethany, OK 73008
(405) 521-0234
24-hour hotline

OREGON

Eugene

Associated Lane Intergency
Rape Team (A.L.I.R.T.)
125 E. 8th, Rm. 170
Eugene, OR 97401
(503) 687-4478
(information line only)

Portland

Rape Victim Advocate Project
Multnomah County District
Attorney
804 Multnomah County
Courthouse
Portland, OR 97204
(503) 248-5059
24-hour services

Salem

Women's Crisis Service
P.O. Box 851
Salem, OR 97308
(503) 399-7722 (hotline)
(503) 378-1572 (office)
24-hour hotline

PENNSYLVANIA

Allentown

Rape Crisis Council of Lehigh
Valley, Inc.
P.O. Box 1445
Allentown, PA 18105
(215) 437-6610 or 437-6611
24-hour hotline

Erie

Erie County Rape Crisis
Center
356 E. 11th St.
Erie, PA 16503
(814) 456-1001 (hotline)
(814) 454-3440 or
455-4560 (office)
9:00 am-5:00 pm
24-hour hotline

Harrisburg

Harrisburg Area Rape Crisis
Center
P.O. Box 38
Harrisburg, PA 17108
(717) 238-7273
24-hour hotline

Johnstown

YWCA Women's Help Center
526 Somerset St.
Johnstown, PA 15901
(814) 536-5361
9:00 am-9:00 pm Mon;
9:00 am-5:00 pm Tues-Fri

Lancaster

Lancaster Rape Aid and
Prevention
2324 Wood St.
Lancaster, PA 17603
(717) 392-7358
24-hour hotline

Philadelphia

Women Organized Against
Rape
1220 Sansom St.
Philadelphia, PA 19107
(215) 922-3434 (hotline)
(215) 922-7400 (office)
9:00 am-5:00 pm
24-hour hotline

Pittsburgh

Pittsburgh Action Against
Rape
211 S. Oakland Ave.
Pittsburgh, PA 15213
(412) 765-2731 (hotline)
(412) 682-0219 (office)
24-hour hotline

Reading

People Against Rape
Box 885
Reading, PA 19603
(215) 372-7273 (hotline)
(215) 372-8425 (office)
24-hour hotline

Scranton

Rape Crisis Program at the
Women's Resource Center
321-315A Bank Towers Bldg.
Scranton, PA 18503
(717) 346-4671
24-hour hotline

West Chester

Rape Crisis Council of Chester
County
Box 738
West Chester, PA 19380
(215) 692-7273
8:30 am-4:30 pm
24-hour hotline

PUERTO RICO

Caparra Heights

Centro De Ayuda a Victimas
de Violacion
Apartado CH-11321
Caparra Heights Station
Caparra Heights, PR 00922
(809) 765-2285 (hotline)
(809) 765-2412 (office)
24-hour hotline

RHODE ISLAND

Newport

Newport County Community
Mental Health Center, Inc.
174 Bellevue Ave.,
P.O. Box 116
Newport, RI 02840
(401) 846-1213
24-hour hotline

Providence

Rhode Island Rape Crisis
Center, Inc.
235 Promenade St., Rm. 202
Providence, RI 02908
(401) 861-4040 (hotline)
(401) 723-3050 (office)
on call 24 hours

SOUTH CAROLINA

Charleston

People Against Rape
54½ Broad St.
Charleston, SC 29401
(803) 722-7273
24-hour hotline

Greenville

Rape Crisis Council of
Greenville, Inc.
703 E. Washington St.
Greenville, SC 29601
(803) 232-8633 or 271-0220
24-hour services

SOUTH DAKOTA

Aberdeen

Aberdeen Area Rape Task Force
620 SE 15th Ave.
Aberdeen, SD 57401
(605) 225-1010 (hotline)
(605) 226-1212 (office)
1:00 pm-9:00 pm Mon-Sat
24-hour hotline

Brookings

Rape Education, Advocacy
and Counseling Team
(REACT)
Brookings Women's Center
802 11th Ave.
Brookings, SD 57006
(605) 688-4518 or
emergency 911 (police)
24-hour hotline

Rapid City

Victim's Assistance Program
Court Services Department
7th Judicial Circuit
703 Adams
Rapid City, SD 57701
(605) 394-2595
8:00 am-5:00 pm

TENNESSEE

Knoxville

Knoxville Rape Crisis Center
P.O. Box 9418
Knoxville, TN 37920
(615) 522-7273 (hotline)
(615) 522-4745 (office)
24-hour hotline

Memphis

Comprehensive Rape Crisis
Program
1177 Madison, Suite 401
Memphis, TN 38104
(901) 528-2161
24-hour hotline

Nashville

Rape and Sexual Abuse Center
of Davidson County
250 Venture Circle
Nashville, TN 37228
Mailing Address:
P.O. Box 12043
Nashville, TN 37212
(615) 327-1110
24-hour hotline

TEXAS

Abilene

Abilene Rape Crisis Center
P.O. Box 122
Abilene, TX 79604
(915) 677-7895
24-hour hotline

Alamo

Mujeres Unidas/Women
Together
701 Bowie St.
Alamo, TX 78516
(519) 781-3399 (hotline)
(512) 383-4959 (office)
24-hour hotline

Amarillo

Rape Crisis and Sexual Abuse
Service
804 S. Bryan, Suite 218
Amarillo, TX 79106
(806) 373-8022
9:00 am-5:00 pm
24-hour hotline

Austin

Texas Rape Prevention and
Control Project
P.O. Box 13072
Austin, TX 78711
(512) 476-9887
8:00 am-5:00 pm

Dallas

Dallas County Rape Crisis
Center
P.O. Box 35728
Dallas, TX 75235
(214) 521-1020
24-hour hotline

El Paso

Rape Crisis Services El Paso
Mental Health/Mental
Retardation
149 N. Raynolds
El Paso, TX 79905
(915) 779-1800 (hotline)
(915) 532-6203 (office)
24-hour hotline

122

Fort Worth

Rape Crisis Support of Tarrant
County
P.O. Box 17083
Fort Worth, TX 76102
(817) 336-3355
24-hour hotline

Houston

Houston Rape Crisis Coalition
Box 4157
Houston, TX 77210
(713) 228-1505
on call 24 hours

Rape Counseling Program
Harris County Health
Department
2370 Rice Blvd.
Houston, TX 77005
(713) 526-8444
8:00 am-5:00 pm
(or by appointment)

Lubbock

Lubbock Rape Crisis Center
P.O. Box 2000
Lubbock, TX 79457
(806) 763-7273 (hotline)
(806) 763-3232 (office)
24-hour hotline

San Antonio

Advocacy Program for
Victims of Crime
Department of Human
Resources and Services
City of San Antonio
P.O. Box 9066
San Antonio, TX 78285
(512) 226-4301
8:00 am-4:30 pm
(also by appointment)

Waco

Waco Rape Crisis Center
P.O. Box 464,
201 W. Waco Drive
Waco, TX 76703
(817) 752-1113
24-hour hotline

UTAH

Moab

Rape Crisis Intervention Team
739 N. 500 W.
Moab, UT 84532
(801) 259-5367
24-hour services

Ogden

YWCA-Women's Crisis
Shelter
505 27th St.
Ogden, UT 84403
(801) 392-7273 (hotline)
(801) 394-9456 (office)
24-hour hotline

Provo

Utah County Rape Crisis Line
P.O. Box 1375
Provo, UT 84601
(801) 375-5111
24-hour hotline

Salt Lake City

The Victim Witness
Counseling Unit
Salt Lake County Attorney's
Office
460 S. 3rd E.
Salt Lake City, UT 84111
(801) 535-5558
8:30 am-5:00 pm

VERMONT

Brattleboro

Women's Crisis Center
67 Main St.
Brattleboro, VT 05301
(802) 254-6954
24-hour hotline

Burlington

Women's Rape Crisis Center
P.O. Box 92
Burlington, VT 05401
(802) 863-1236
24-hour hotline

Rutland

Rutland County Rape Crisis
Team
Box 723
Rutland, VT 05701
(802) 775-1000
24-hour hotline

VIRGINIA

Alexandria

Rape Victim Companion
Program
405 Cameron St.
P.O. Box 178
Alexandria, VA 22313
(703) 768-1400 (hotline)
(703) 750-6631 (office)
9:00 am-5:00 pm
24-hour hotline

Arlington

Arlington County Rape Victim
Companion Service
1725 N. George Mason Dr.
Arlington, VA 22205
(703) 527-4077 (hotline)
(703) 558-2815 (office)
8:30 am-5:00 pm
24-hour hotline

Charlottesville

Charlottesville Rape Crisis Group
214 Rugby Rd.
Charlottesvile, VA 22901
(804) 977-7273
24-hour hotline

124

IF SHE IS RAPED

Norfolk

Tidewater Rape Information
Service, Inc.(TRIS)
230 W. Bute St.
Norfolk, VA 23510
(804) 622-4300
24-hour hotline

Richmond

Crisis Intervention Program
102 N. Belvidere St.
Richmond, VA 23220
(804) 648-9224
24-hour hotline

Roanoke

TRUST, The Roanoke Valley
Trouble Center
3515 Williamson Rd.
Roanoke, VA 24012
(703) 563-0311 (hotline)
(703) 345-8859 (office)
24-hour hotline

WASHINGTON

Olympia

Thurston County Rape Relief
YWCA
220 E. Union Ave.
Olympia, WA 98501
(206) 352-2211 (hotline)
(206) 352-0593 (office)
8:00 am-5:00 pm Mon-Fri
24-hour hotline

Pullman

Pullman Rape Resource Line
CUB Student Activities Center
Washington State University
Pullman, WA 99163
(509) 332-4357
24-hour hotline

Seattle

Seattle Rape Relief
4224 University Way, NE
Seattle, WA 98105
(206) 632-7273
24-hour hotline

Spokane

Rape Crisis Network
N. 1226 Howard St.
Spokane, WA 99201
(509) 624-7273
8:30 am-5:00 pm
24-hour hotline

Tacoma

Pierce County Rape Relief
Allenmore Medical Center
Suite A105
S. 19th & Union
Tacoma, WA 98405
(206) 627-1135
8:00 am-4:30 pm
24-hour hotline

Wenatchee

Wenatchee Rape Crisis Center
Chelan County Special
Services Center
327 Okanogan St.
Wenatchee, WA 98801
(509) 663-7446
9:00 am-5:30 pm
24-hour hotline

Yakima

Central Washington
Comprehensive Mental Health
Center Rape Relief Program
321 E. Yakima Ave.
P.O. Box 959
Yakima, WA 98907
(509) 575-4200
9:00 am-5:00 pm
24-hour hotline

WEST VIRGINIA

Charleston

Sexual Assault Information
Center, Inc.
1036 Quarrier St., #317
Charleston, WV 25301
(304) 344-9834 (hotline)
(304) 344-9839 (office)
9:00 am-5:00 pm
24-hour hotline

Huntington

Community Mental Health
Center, Region II
3375 Rt. 60 E.
Huntington, WV 25705
(304) 525-7851
24-hour hotline

Morgantown

Rape and Domestic Violence
Information Center
P.O. Box 4228
Morgantown, WV 26505
(304) 599-6800
9:00 am-5:00 pm
24-hour hotline

Parkersburg

Rape Information and
Counseling Service
P.O. Box 2033
Parkersburg, WV 26101
(304) 485-9700
24-hour hotline

WISCONSIN

Green Bay

Green Bay Rape Crisis Center,
Ltd.
744 S. Webster,
P.O. Box 1700
Green Bay, WI 54305
(414) 468-3553
24-hour hotline

La Crosse

New Horizons-YWCA
Women's Center
P.O. Box 2031
LaCrosse, WI 54601
(608) 784-6419
24-hour hotline

Madison

Dane County Project on Rape
120 W. Mifflin St.
Madison, WI 53703
(608) 251-5440
10:00 am-2:00 pm
(or by appointment)
24-hour advocate services

Milwaukee

Women's Crisis Line
1428 N. Farwell Ave.
Milwaukee, WI 53202
(414) 964-7535 (hotline)
(414) 271-8112 (office)
24-hour hotline

Oshkosh

Winnebago County Rape
Crisis Center
404 N. Main St.
Oshkosh, WI 54901
(414) 426-1460
24-hour hotline

Racine

Women's Resource Center
740 College Ave.
Racine, WI 53403
(414) 633-3233
24-hour hotline

Stevens Point

Women's Resource Center, Inc.
2101A Main St.
Stevens Point, WI 54481
(715) 346-4851

Wausau

Domestic Abuse and Sexual
Assault Victim
Services, Inc. (D.A.S.A.V.S.)
P.O. Box 172
Wausau, WI 54401
(715) 842-7323 (hotline)
(715) 842-7636 (office)
9:00 am-4:00 pm
24-hour hotline

WYOMING

Jackson

Western Wyoming Mental
Health Association
115 W. Snowking Ave.
P.O. Box 1868
Jackson, WY 83001
(307) 733-2046
(800) 442-6383 (toll-free)
24-hour emergency services

Rocksprings

Sweetwater County Task
Force on Sexual Assault
450 S. Main
Rocksprings, WY 82901
(307) 382-4381
9:00 am-5:00 pm

CANADA

ALBERTA

Edmonton

Rape Crisis Centre of Edmonton
416-10010-105 St.
Edmonton, Alberta, Canada
T5J 1C4
(403) 429-0023
24-hour hotline

BRITISH COLUMBIA

Naniamo

Naniamo Rape Relief Centre
361 Vancouver Ave.
Naniamo, British Columbia,
Canada V9S 4G3
(604) 753-0022 (hotline)
(604) 753-1021 (office)
9:30 am-5:30 pm
24-hour hotline

Vancouver

Vancouver Anti-Sexual
Assault Centre
4-45 Kingsway
Vancouver, British Columbia,
Canada V5T 3H7
(604) 732-1613 (hotline)
10:00 am-5:00 pm
24-hour hotline

MANATOBA

Winnipeg

Rape Crisis and Information
Centre (Klinic, Inc.)
545 Broadway Ave.
Winnipeg, Manitoba,
Canada R3C 0W3
(204) 774-4525 (hotline)
(204) 786-6943 (office)
24-hour hotline

NEW BRUNSWICK

Fredericton

Fredericton Rape Crisis
Service
P.O. Box 1033
Fredericton, New Brunswick,
Canada E3B 5C2
(506) 454-0437
24-hour hotline

NEWFOUNDLAND

St. John's

St. John's Rape Crisis and
Information Centre
P.O. Box 6072
St. John's, Newfoundland,
Canada A1C 5X8
(709) 726-1411 (hotline)
(709) 753-0220 (office)
24-hour hotline

ONTARIO

Guelph

Women in Crisis University
of Guelph
P.O. Box 43
U.G.C.S.A.
Guelph, Ontario,
Canada N1G 2V7
(519) 836-5710
24-hour hotline

Niagara Falls

CARSA Niagara Region
Sexual Assault Centre
5017 Victoria Ave.
Niagara Falls, Ontario,
Canada L2E 4C9
(416) 356-9662
24-hour hotline

Ottawa

Ottawa Rape Crisis Centre
P.O. Box 35, Station B
Ottawa, Ontario, Canada
(613) 238-6666 (hotline)
(613) 238-6667 (office)
24-hour hotline

Thunder Bay

Thunder Bay Rape and
Sexual Assault Centre
316 Bay St.
P.O. Box 314 TBF
Thunder Bay, Ontario, Canada
(807) 344-4502

Toronto

Toronto Rape Crisis Centre
Box 6597, Postal Station A
Toronto, Ontario,
Canada M5W 1X4
(416) 964-8080 (hotline)
(416) 964-7477 (office)
24-hour hotline

Windsor

Sexual Assault Crisis Clinic
Windsor Western Hospital
Out-Patient Clinics
Windsor, Ontario,
Canada N9C 3Z4
(519) 253-9667 (hotline)
(519) 253-4261,
ext. 298 (office)
24-hour hotline

QUEBEC

Montreal

Montreal Women's Aid
C.P. 82, Station E
Montreal, Quebec, Canada
(514) 270-8291
24-hour hotline

SASKATCHEWAN

Regina

Regina Women's Community
Centre and Rape Crisis Line
1810 Smith St., Rm. 219
Regina, Saskatchewan,
Canada S4P 1X7
(306) 352-0434
24-hour hotline

Appendix C
Suggested Readings

Amir, M. *Patterns of forcible rape*. Chicago: University of Chicago Press, 1971.

Brodyaga, L., Gates, M., Singer, S., Tucker, M., & White, R. *Rape and its victims: A report for citizens, health facilities, and criminal justice agencies*. Washington, D.C.: U.S. Department of Justice, 1975.

Brownmiller, S. *Against our will: Men, women and rape*. New York: Bantam Books, 1975.

Burgess, A. W., & Holmstrom, L. L. *Rape: Crisis and recovery*. Bowie, MD: Robert J. Brady Co., 1979.

Burgess, A. W., Groth, A. N., Holmstrom, L. L., & Sgroi, S. M. *Sexual assault of children and adolescents*. Lexington, MA: Lexington Books, 1978.

Burgess, A. W., & Holmstrom, L. L. *The victim of rape: Institutional reaction*. New York: John Wiley & Sons, 1978.

Castleman, M. *Sexual solutions.* New York: Simon & Schuster, 1980.

Chappell, D., Geis, R., & Geis, G. (Eds.) *Forcible rape.* New York: Columbia University Press, 1977.

Connell, N., & Wilson, C., (Eds.) *Rape: The first sourcebook for women.* New York: New American Library, 1974.

Erickson, E., McEvoy, A., & Colucci, N. *Child abuse and neglect: A guidebook for educators and community leaders* (2nd Ed.). Holmes Beach, FL: Learning Publications, 1984.

Gager, N., & Schurr, C. *Sexual assault: Confronting rape in America.* New York: Grosset & Dunlap, 1976.

Goodwin, J. *Sexual abuse: Incest victims and their families.* Boston: John Wright & PSG, Inc., 1982.

Griffin, S. *Rape: The power of consciousness.* San Francisco, CA: Harper & Row, 1979.

Holstrom, L. & Burgess, A. *The victim of rape.* New Brunswick, NJ: Transaction Books, 1983.

Johnson, K. M. *If you are raped.* Holmes Beach, FL: Learning Publications, 1984.

Katz, S., & Mazur, M. A. *Understanding the rape victim.* New York: John Wiley & Sons, 1979.

Mayer, A. *Incest: A treatment manual for therapy with victims, spouses, and offenders.* Holmes Beach, FL: Learning Publications, 1983.

Sanders, W. *Rape and woman's identity.* Beverly Hills, CA: Sage Publications, 1980.

Scacco, A. M., Jr. (Ed.) *Male rape: A casebook of sexual aggressions.* New York: AMS Press, Inc., 1982.

Schwendinger, J. R., & Schwendinger, H. *Rape and inequality.* Beverly Hills, CA: Sage Publications, 1983.

Sgroi, S. *Handbook of clinical intervention in child sexual abuse.* Lexington, MA: Lexington Books, 1982.

Storaska, F. *How to say no to a rapist . . . and survive.* New York: Random House, 1975.

Thorman, G. *Incestuous families.* Springfield, IL: Charles C. Thomas, 1983.

U.S. Department of Human Services *Sexual abuse of children.* Washington, D.C., 1980.

Index

HV 6558 .M33 1984

DATE DUE

Demco, Inc. 38-293